Tell me about the Holy Spirit

How to be filled with love, joy, peace and power
and extend the Kingdom of God.

Arnold V Page

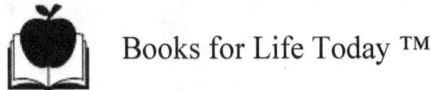
Books for Life Today ™

What people have said

Tell me about the Holy Spirit has left me convicted and eager to walk more closely in step with the Spirit, open to what He intends to do in and through me.
    Andy Geers, Creator of the PrayerMate app and nephew of the author

I enjoyed reading this book and can highly recommend it. It is a must read for the sceptic, but also for those who believe that they have received the Holy Spirit and yet lack the full experience as evidenced in the Acts of the Apostles. So many claim to have received the Holy Spirit, yet lack any real evidence. This book will help them to find what they are searching for.
    Rev. David Hathaway DD President Eurovision Mission to Europe

Mr Page has written a powerful book on the Holy Spirit. From who the Holy Spirit is, to what He does and why believers cannot function as true believers without Him, this book tells it all. If you are hungry for more of God, more of His power, presence and presents, this is the resource you need.
    Leke Sanusi, Head, Redeemed Christian Church of God Mission, UK.

Finally, a book that is easy to read, flows nicely, and seeks to help the reader find ways not just to get to know about the Holy Spirit but to encounter Him. It is hard to believe that a comprehensive ideology of the Holy Spirit could be so eloquently delivered in such a small book.
    Rev. Scott Pash, Minister of Elim Hope Church, Lane End

Brilliantly clear and concise practical Biblical teaching.
    Paul Harvey, Buckinghamshire

This is the best book on the Holy Spirit that I have ever read. Brilliant!
    Rev. Gregory Hargrove JP, retired Free Methodist minister

Copyright © 2021 by Arnold V Page

The right of Arnold V Page to be identified as the author of this work has been asserted by him in the United Kingdom in accordance with The Copyright, Designs and Patents Act 1988.

Except as provided by The Copyright Act 1956, The Copyright, Designs and Patents Act 1988, and The Copyright and Related Rights Regulations 2003, no part of this publication may be reproduced, stored in a retrieval system, or transmitted in any form or by any means without the prior written permission of the copyright owner.

Revised Standard Version
Bible verses are taken from the Revised Standard Version of the Bible, © 1946, 1952 and 1971, the Division of Christian Education of the National Council of the Churches of Christ in the United States of America. All rights reserved.

British Library Cataloguing-in-Publication Data.
A catalogue record for this book is available from the British Library.

Notes
British spelling (e.g. 'centre', 'colour', 'favourite', 'judgement') has been used.
When referring to a man or a woman I have generally used the masculine pronoun to mean either, in accordance with historical practice and grammatical correctness.

First edition

ISBN: 978-1-91612-135-5 (Paperback)
ISBN: 978-1-91612-136-2 (Epub)
ASIN: B09F25G24X (Kindle)

 Books for Life Today™
86A Totteridge Lane, High Wycombe, HP13 7PN, England
Website: booksforlife.today
Email: sales@booksforlife.today

Preface

In these last-remaining years before the Lord Jesus returns as king, those of us who believe in him must dedicate ourselves without reservation to the mission Jesus gave us of proclaiming him as Saviour and Lord. We are all different, and we can all engage in this task in different ways, but however we do it we have all been promised a helper – the Holy Spirit. Jesus gave this promise to his first disciples, but in St Peter's first public sermon he said it is for every subsequent believer too, including you and me.

Every new missionary advance made by the early church was initiated by the direct intervention of the Holy Spirit.

At 9 o'clock in the morning on the day of Pentecost AD 30, the Holy Spirit fell upon Jesus's first disciples. They all began to talk at once, praising the mighty works of God in a range of foreign languages corresponding to the languages of the foreign pilgrims who had come to Jerusalem for the festival.

I imagine that the disciples then went out into the streets still praising God, so that a huge crowd gathered round them to listen. And because what they heard was so amazing, the people listened to Peter's explanation. He told them that the scriptures had prophesied this event, and that they had also prophesied the death and resurrection of Jesus Christ, something Peter and the other disciples had directly witnessed.

Peter went on to accuse the Jewish religious leaders and the population of Jerusalem as a whole of collaborating in the crucifixion of God's promised Saviour, implying that unless they immediately sought for God's forgiveness and put their trust in Jesus as Lord and Saviour they would be in serious trouble. The crowds believed him. Three thousand people committed their lives to Jesus as their promised Messiah, and the church was born. It was a fulfilment of Jesus's promise,

"When [the Counsellor] *comes, he will convince the world concerning sin and righteousness and judgement."*

Some time later, Peter, encouraged by three visions from heaven, broke through the rigid Jewish cultural barriers and entered the house of a Gentile Roman centurion in the ancient port of Caesarean. There he spoke about Jesus's ministry, death, resurrection and coming judgement. While he was still speaking, the Holy Spirit fell upon Cornelius and his entire household. They too burst out in praises to God, some of them at least in other languages as the first disciples had done. And that was how Peter and the believers with him discovered with amazement that God wanted Gentiles as well as Jews to come into his kingdom.

By AD 48 there was already an established church with prophets and teachers as far north as Antioch, a town in modern Syria. One day *'while they were worshipping the Lord and fasting, the Holy Spirit said, "Set apart for me Barnabas and Saul for the work to which I have called them."'* (Acts 13:2) Obeying this groundbreaking command, the two men took the gospel to Cyprus and Asia Minor, founding churches in what is now southern Turkey.

Four years later Saul, now called Paul, was back in Asia Minor, but this time he and his companions didn't seem to be having much success. The reason for this was that the Holy Spirit had more important plans for them:

> They went through the region of Phrygia and Galatia, having been forbidden by the Holy Spirit to speak the word in Asia. And when they had come opposite Mysia, they attempted to go into Bithynia but the Spirit of Jesus did not allow them; so, passing by Mysia, they went down to Troas.
>
> Acts 16:6-10

From Troas there was only a short sea-crossing to Europe, and in Troas Paul had a vision of a man pleading with him to come over to Macedonia, which was then a Roman province directly to the north of

Greece. Thus, under the direction of the Holy Spirit, the gospel reached Europe! First Israel, then Syria, then Turkey and finally Europe. All within twenty years!

Furthermore, the New Testament makes it crystal clear that the main reason thousands of people believed in Jesus so early on was that when the apostles and others proclaimed Jesus's resurrection and God's appointment of him as Lord and Saviour, the Holy Spirit confirmed they were speaking the truth by means of miraculous signs. St Mark tells us that *'they went forth and preached everywhere, while the Lord worked with them and confirmed the message by the signs that attended it.'*

For example, Peter and John healed a man who'd been unable to walk since birth. When they told the crowd of people who gathered round that it was through faith in Jesus that he had been healed, many of the onlookers became Jesus's disciples. Luke tells us that the number of Jewish men who believed in Jesus as God's promised Messiah increased to five thousand.

Philip was supposed to be a deacon helping with the daily distribution of food to widows, but he went off to Samaria and preached to them about Jesus. When he did this, evil spirits came out of many who were possessed, crying with a loud voice, and many paralysed and lame people were healed. The result was that *'the multitudes with one accord gave heed to what was said by Philip, when they heard him and saw the signs which he did.'*

As a final example of the Holy Spirit's essential role in the spread of the Christian faith, Paul looked back on his ministry and wrote about *'what Christ has wrought through me to win obedience from the Gentiles, by word and deed, by the power of signs and wonders, by the power of the Holy Spirit.'*

Whether they were Jews, Samaritans or Gentiles, people turned to the Lord because of two things: the proclamation of Jesus Christ, risen from the dead to be Lord and Saviour; and the Holy Spirit's confirmation of that message by the miracles that accompanied it.

If there is to be a significant missionary advance in your local church and neighbourhood, it will only be through a new encounter with the Spirit of Mission. When we pray for God's kingdom to come, you and I are supposed to be part of the answer. We must repent of our lack of faith, obedience and love, and pray, "Come, Holy Spirit," because without his help we are powerless. Pray this for yourself, for your church leaders if necessary, and for your whole church. Find people to pray with you. Pray!

Both the scriptures and current world events point to Christ's imminent return. We don't have much longer to earn Jesus's accolade, *"Well done, good and faithful servant... Enter into the joy of your master."* So wake up, people of God! *"You shall receive power when the Holy Spirit has come upon you and you shall be my witnesses..."*

I know you and I can't literally be witnesses to Christ's resurrection, but we can still tell people it happened, and his promise of the Holy Spirit's help to do this is for us all. *"For the promise is to you and to your children, and to all that are far off, every one whom the Lord our God calls to him."* So ask the Lord to fulfil that promise in you and keep asking him to do it until he does!

Arnold V Page, High Wycombe, England, September 2021

Acknowledgements

I am grateful to all my friends who provided helpful comments and corrections to this book and its cover, particularly to David Marsh for his literary criticism, and to Andrew Farrer, who can perceive a mote where I don't notice even a beam.

Contents

Introduction 1
Chapter 1: The Spirit leads us to Christ 5
Chapter 2: He restores our spirits to life 11
Chapter 3: He enables us to live as Jesus lived on earth 19
Chapter 4: How can I receive the Holy Spirit? 31
Chapter 5: Overcoming evil 43
Chapter 6: Assurance and worship 53
Chapter 7: The fruit of the Spirit 67
Chapter 8: Empowered to do God's will 73
Chapter 9: Some questions about speaking in tongues 83
Chapter 10: How can I continue to be filled with the Holy Spirit? 91
Chapter 11: Ruled by the Spirit 95
Epilogue 103
Other books by Arnold V Page 107
About the author 111

x

Introduction

"Oh, Arnold, what shall we do?"

It was 3 a.m. on August 19th, 1969, and my wife Ann couldn't sleep. We were both in the kitchen, looking for something to eat, and having no idea where we could turn to for help. My first appointment as a Methodist minister on probation was proving desperately tough, and coping with our first baby was stretching Ann's patience and strength to breaking point. She couldn't sleep properly, she felt tired all the time, and all her love for life had disappeared. Her strong faith in God was fast evaporating.

The previous day I had told a fellow minister I was praying for the Holy Spirit, because there was none of the fruit of the Spirit such as love, joy and peace in my life. He told me something of his own experience of the Spirit, and he also said that when people are in a state of depression, evil spirits can sometimes take hold of them so that the depression becomes spiritual as well physical.

We came out of the kitchen.

"Let's read something from the Bible," I suggested.

We sat down together on the old settee which the church had provided along with the rest of our furniture, and I turned to the book of Psalms. I began to read from the first one I found:

Bless the Lord, O my soul; and all that is within me, bless his holy name! Bless the Lord, O my soul, and forget not all his benefits, who forgives all your iniquity, who heals all your diseases, who redeems your life from the pit, who crowns you with steadfast love and mercy, who satisfies you with good as long as you live so that your youth is renewed like the eagle's...

Psalm 103:1-5

It is hard to explain, but it was as though God was speaking to us personally. Somewhat awestruck, we returned to our separate bedrooms. (Earlier in the night, when Ann was tossing and turning, I had moved into the spare bedroom to get some sleep myself.) In my heart there was a wonderful sense of reassurance and gratitude to God for the amazing way he had encouraged us through the words of the Psalm.

But gradually my worries and fears returned. I thought not just about my churches, but other churches; then people not in any church, and then people in the factories where I had worked. And it seemed to me that everybody I thought of was fast bound by dark powers of evil. It seemed almost impossible that I would ever find rest in the company of people who had been set free from sin and were rejoicing in the life of the Kingdom of Heaven.

And then it occurred to me that a sense of despair like this always came to me at the same time as it came to Ann, as if Satan suddenly remembered us and set one of his servants on both of us at once. I wasn't sure I even believed in evil spirits, but this thought was so strong that I decided to do what our minister friend had recommended in the afternoon. I spoke aloud some Bible verses that seemed relevant: *'Perfect love casts out fear'*, *'Now is the prince of this world cast out'*, and two others. And I said, with as much authority as I could muster, "In the name of Jesus, I command you to depart!" I sensed that Jesus's name was quite sufficient to dispatch any evil spirits in terror. And as soon as I had said those words, I thought I heard Ann crying.

I lifted my head from the pillow to hear her more clearly. It sounded as though she was speaking to someone, or even that several people were speaking. I thought God must be casting an evil spirit out of her. Moments later she came into my room, and I switched the light on. She looked very shaken. "What has happened to me?" she asked.

"It's all right," I said reassuringly. "I think an evil spirit has come out of you."

"Oh no, it wasn't anything nasty," she replied. "It was wonderful! I came back to bed and read two pages of the book I'm reading. Then I lay down, and I thought of the lovely words God had spoken to us. Suddenly my mind seemed to be full of light. I began to thank him, but it was in some other language. I spoke quietly at first under the bedclothes because I didn't want you to hear me, but then I sat up and spoke more loudly. I could have gone on longer, but I thought I'd better come and tell you what was happening."

If anyone had ever looked agog, it was I at that moment. "You must have been speaking in tongues then!" was my astonished reply.

Neither of us had ever heard of someone speaking in tongues outside the New Testament, so this was gobsmacking news, or it would have been if the word had been in current use back then. Someone actually speaking in tongues as the first disciples did on the day of Pentecost was a total miracle!

Later that morning my once depressed wife was singing one of the loveliest songs I had ever heard, with both words and music given by the Holy Spirit. She discovered she could praise God in tongues whenever she wanted to, and within a few days she was receiving incredibly beautiful words of prophecy from the Lord. He had answered my prayers for the Holy Spirit, but he had got the wrong person!

A week before all this happened, two kind friends had let us spend a couple of days in their seaside flat in Sheringham, to give us a break and help Ann climb out of her depression. The break had done nothing to help. But two days after the Lord filled her with his Spirit, a lady stopped me in the street.

"I've just been talking to your wife," she said. "My goodness, her holiday's done her a world of good. She is like a new person!"

Chapter 1: The Spirit leads us to Christ.

The Lord Jesus promised that the Holy Spirit would lead us into all the truth. Therefore, my purpose is to introduce you to the Holy Spirit and his ministry, for once the Spirit has taken up residence he will – in time – teach you everything you need to know about God and how he wants you to live and serve him. You will still need the Bible, and you'll still need to be part of a living church, for these are the chief means the Holy Spirit uses to teach us the truth that brings us to fullness of spiritual life. However, to understand and accept and live by the teachings of the Bible and the church, we all need the help of the Spirit. *"He will guide you into all the truth... He will take what is mine and declare it to you."* (John 16:13,14)

The Holy Spirit is more than a mysterious power: he is a personal manifestation of the one creator God. Just as the chemical H_2O can appear as solid ice, liquid water or gaseous steam, so God has revealed himself to us as the Father, Son and Holy Spirit, all apparently very different but all essentially the same unique God. That's why he said in Genesis chapter 1, *"Let us make man in our image."* The Hebrew word for God, *Elohim*, is plural.

This book began life as a message from the end of the earth, for I wrote the first draft in the Chilean city of Punta Arenas, the most southerly mainland city in the world. In Punta Arenas Methodist Church, there was a young lady whose father rarely attended the services. He was rebellious towards God and resentful of any attempt to change his attitude. His daughter Valeria had been almost stone deaf in one ear for many years. One day she was healed by prayer to the Lord Jesus. I know this is true because it was my wife and I who prayed for her. Her father came to church the following Sunday and publicly gave thanks for what God had done for his daughter, by playing three hymns of praise on his harmonica! Two months later, when Hector himself had to go into hospital for a long-awaited operation in Santiago, he testified about Jesus Christ to every other patient in his ward. Three of them were healed, partly or fully, through his prayers for them, and they gave their lives to Christ! Hector himself never had his operation: a pre-op scan showed that the gallstones which had been blocking him up had disappeared!

In this story we can see how a gift of the Holy Spirit – in this case the gift of healing – brought several people to Christ where previously men's efforts alone had failed.

The first and most important thing the Holy Spirit wants to do in a person's life is to lead him to Christ. He wants to lead everyone to a place where they recognize their need for Christ's help and are willing to accept it on Christ's terms. That is what Jesus meant when He said of the Spirit, *"He will glorify me."* (John 16:14) Today he might have said, "He will advertise me."

The ideal advertisement does three things:

- it arrests people's attention, even if they have had no prior interest in the product or service concerned;
- it highlights a need or awakens a desire which it offers to satisfy;
- it convinces them it can meet that need or satisfy that desire better than anything else can – or preferably that it is the only thing that can do this.

The world's greatest need is for the life which only Jesus Christ can give. War, violence, oppression, injustice, robbery, poverty, family breakdown, personal breakdown, disease and death: these are all the consequences of what the Bible calls sin. Sin has affected man's nature in such a way that he can no longer live at peace with God or his fellow man. Furthermore, the Bible makes it absolutely clear that sin is the sole cause of physical death. As I revise this book in 2021, the world is battling against an invisible enemy in the form of a coronavirus, Covid-19. Thousands of people are dying of it every day. Yet far, far more serious is this other invisible enemy, a spiritual disease which will kill us all if we do not turn to Jesus to be rescued from it. It is the disease of sin.

A new life, free from sin and its effects, is what God is offering through his Son Jesus Christ. Jesus himself first demonstrated the unique quality of such a life as a man. Then, after his return to Heaven, the Holy Spirit took over the task of advertising it to the world through the lives of his followers.

In the early days of the church, we see the Spirit arresting people's attention by means of miracles, and by visibly demonstrating what Jesus could do for everyone who believed in him.

> "[This great salvation] *was declared at first by the Lord, and it was attested to us by those who heard him, while God also bore witness by signs and wonders and various miracles and by gifts of the Holy Spirit...*"
>
> (Hebrews 2:3,4)

The young Christian church grew with phenomenal rapidity. Only thirty years or so after Christ's death and resurrection in Jerusalem, the historian Tacitus could write of 'an immense multitude' of Christians as far away as Rome. When the comparative speed of travel in those days is taken into account, this was equivalent to the other side of the world today.

It was not that the inhabitants of the Roman Empire found it easy to believe the Christian message. Preaching Christ crucified was '*a stumbling block to Jews and folly to Gentiles.*' (1 Corinthians 1:23) How could Jews believe in a Messiah who got himself killed, when their scriptures had promised he would reign for ever? How could Greeks believe that any god would condescend to get himself born as a human baby in a cattle shed? How could Romans believe that the son of a Jewish carpenter whom they had sentenced to death was mightier than Caesar?

The Christian message is just as incredible to any natural mind today. We are asking people to believe that:

- the God who made the universe in a manner contrary to almost every scientific belief was somehow born on the earth as a man
- he was the promised Saviour and King of the Jewish race but then deliberately got himself killed
- he miraculously returned to life and disappeared into the sky with a promise to bring all his followers back to life in the same way for ever
- he will return with a host of angels to rule this present earth for a thousand years
- he will then restore to conscious life everybody else who has ever lived without knowing him or trusting in him, either for everlasting life or for fitting punishment and final death, depending on what they have done
- and finally, that this same Jesus will then reign for ever in a completely new earth which God will make, where those to whom he grants everlasting life will live happily in recreated bodies which will never die again.

It is going to take more than mere words to get anyone today to believe the full gospel as told in the Bible from Genesis chapter 1 to Revelation chapter 22!

The first Christians did have more than mere words to do the job. Jews, Greeks and Romans believed what they preached because the Holy Spirit supplied visible proof of its truth. As Paul wrote, *'Our gospel came to you not only in word, but also in power and in the Holy Spirit and with full conviction.'* (1 Thessalonians 1:5) The primary purpose of the supernatural gifts of the Holy Spirit is not to bless believers but to convince unbelievers. (Mark 16:15-20; Acts 1:8)

Almost without exception, whenever we read in the New Testament of people being converted to Christ, it is after some demonstration of God's power. (Acts chapters 2 to 5; Acts 8:6,7,12)

As an example, let's look at Acts 9:32-35. In Lydda, Peter came across a man named Aeneas who was paralysed and had been bedridden for eight years. *'And Peter said to him, "Aeneas, Jesus Christ heals you; rise and make your bed." And immediately he rose. And all the residents of Lydda and Sharon saw him, and they turned to the Lord.'* You see the effectiveness of the Holy Spirit's evangelistic method? The entire city of Lydda and even the neighbouring city of Sharon were converted to the Lord through the healing of one man! Lydda and Sharon were probably only what we would call villages; nevertheless, that was a mighty impressive outcome.

However, signs alone do not lead people to believe in Jesus Christ. They are given to confirm that the spoken message of Christ's death and resurrection and his appointment by God as Lord and Saviour is true. *"Jesus Christ heals you,"* Peter said, *'...and they turned to the Lord.'* The purpose of supernatural signs is to confirm what an evangelist says. The evangelist's words should also be supported and confirmed by the life he lives – itself a gift of the Holy Spirit. In effect, the Spirit uses three principal means to convince people of their need of Christ:

- the evangelist's words
- supernatural signs and wonders
- the life of the evangelist and of the church as a whole

Thus, Paul writes:

...how are they to believe in him of whom they have never heard? And how are they to hear without a preacher? Romans 10:14

...what Christ has wrought through me to win obedience from the Gentiles by word and deed, by the power of signs and wonders, by the power of the Holy Spirit...   Romans 15:18,19

For you remember our labour and toil, brethren; we worked night and day, that we might not burden any one of you, while we preached to you the gospel of God. You are witnesses, and God also, how holy and righteous and blameless was our behaviour...   1 Thessalonians 2:9,10

By these three means the Holy Spirit convinces people that they are separated from God by sin, and that God will judge and condemn them to final death unless they learn to live righteously as he wants them to. Jesus said, *"When [the Spirit] comes, he will convince the world concerning sin and righteousness and judgement."* (John 16:8) And when he has done that, the Spirit convinces them that the only way to live righteously is to repent of their sin, to trust in Jesus Christ as Saviour, to obey him as Lord, and to receive the promised help of the Spirit himself.

Chapter 2: He restores our spirits to life.

Because of sin, our spirits are dead to God. We cannot understand the things of God, nor live as he wants us to, even if we try.

...you were dead through the trespasses and sins in which you once walked...   Ephesians 2:1,2

The unspiritual man does not receive the gifts of the Spirit of God, for they are folly to him, and he is not able to understand them because they are spiritually discerned.   1 Corinthians 2:14

...the god of this world has blinded the minds of the unbelievers, to keep them from seeing the light of the gospel...   2 Corinthians 4:4

I can will what is right but I cannot do it. For I do not do the good I want, but the evil I do not want is what I do.   Romans 7:18,19

The spiritual disease of sin is something we inherit from Adam. Like the corona virus, it has spread throughout the world. 'Therefore as sin came into the world through one man and death through sin, and so death spread to all men because all men sinned...' (Romans 5:12) Jesus however was born of the Spirit of God, so he was the son of God rather than the son of Adam, and therefore he was free from sin. "*...do not fear to take Mary your wife, for that which is conceived in her is of the Holy Spirit.*" (Matthew 1:20) 'And the angel said to her, *'The Holy Spirit will come upon you, and the power of the Most High will overshadow you; therefore the child to be born will be called holy, the Son of God."* (Luke 1:35)

Jesus said that to live in the kingdom of God we must be born again, this time of the Spirit of God. *'Truly, truly, I say to you, unless one is born* anew, he cannot see the kingdom of God." (John 3:3) How does this happen? Jesus hinted at the answer in his continuing conversation with the Pharisee Nicodemus: *"Truly, truly, I say to you, unless one is born of water and the Spirit, he cannot enter the kingdom of God. That which is born of the flesh is flesh, and that which is born of the Spirit is spirit."* (John 3:5,6) Jesus was contrasting natural and spiritual birth, explaining that while we were all born naturally, we also need to be reborn spiritually in order to enter God's everlasting kingdom. The question is how? How are we born again? The clue is in Jesus's words about being born of water and the Spirit.

Centuries earlier, the prophet Ezekiel received this promise for Israel from God:

> *"I will sprinkle clean water upon you, and you shall be clean from all your uncleannesses, and from all your idols I will cleanse you. A new heart I will give you, and a new spirit I will put within you; and I will take out of your flesh the heart of stone and give you a heart of flesh. And I will put my spirit within you, and cause you to walk in my statutes and be careful to observe my ordinances."*   Ezekiel 36:25-27

By means of water God was going to cleanse his people from their sin and idolatry and give them a new spirit of love and obedience. The spirit of God himself would come to live within them to enable them to live as he intended.

John the Baptist proclaimed that Jesus would fulfil this prophecy. *"I baptize you with water for repentance, but he who is coming after me is mightier than I, whose sandals I am not worthy to carry; he will baptize you with the Holy Spirit and with fire."* (Matthew 3:11) Once again John spoke of water and the Spirit of God.

Wherever the word 'baptize' occurs in the New Testament, it means 'immerse', either in water or in the Holy Spirit. That's what the Greek word *baptizo* means: immerse. The correct translation of John the

Baptist's words is, *"I immerse you in water for repentance... he will immerse you in the Holy Spirit and fire."* Fire burns up rubbish. So John told people to be immersed in water to demonstrate their repentance from their past sins, and to be immersed in the Holy Spirit to purify them from present sin and make them holy.

When Jesus said that to enter God's kingdom we must be born of water and the Spirit I suggest he had those words of Ezekiel and John in mind. Peter's speech to the crowds on the day of Pentecost confirms this. When they asked Peter and the other apostles what they must do to be saved from God's anger at their collaboration in the death of Jesus, Peter did not use the words, *"You must be born again."* Instead, he said, *"Repent, and be baptized* (immersed in water) *for the forgiveness of your sins; and you shall receive the gift of the Holy Spirit."* (Acts 2:37,38) There is absolutely no doubt: that is how we are born again, or at least that is God's intention.

So the Bible teaches us that there are three conditions for this new birth to take place in us:

(i) <u>Repent</u>

To repent is to acknowledge we are sinners who have not lived as God intended us to, and to seek his help to put things right. It is to *believe* what God has told us in his Word, and to *do* what he has told us to do in his Word, with the help he offers us through Jesus Christ. The Greek word for repentance means to change our mind, in other words to give up unbelief, and instead to believe what God says. The Latin word for repentance means to change direction, to stop walking away from God in rebellion and disobedience, and instead to walk towards him and live the way he wants us to, now and in the future. Repentance is the first step in being born again. *"The time is fulfilled, and the kingdom of God is at hand; repent, and believe in the gospel."* (Mark 1:15) *"Unless you repent you will all likewise perish."* (Luke

13:5) *"Then to the Gentiles also God has granted repentance unto life."* (Acts 10:18)

(ii) <u>Believe</u>

We must believe in Jesus Christ as Saviour and Lord. To believe in him as *Saviour* is to believe that he alone made it possible for our sins to be forgiven, that he alone can enable us to live without sin, and therefore that he alone can save us from final death. To believe in him as *Lord* is to commit ourselves to live from henceforth in obedience to him and his teaching. Obedience to Jesus is at the heart of discipleship. *"Why do you call me, 'Lord, Lord', and not do what I tell you?"* (Luke 6:46) New birth involves both faith and obedience: *'To all who received him* (as Lord of their lives), *who believed in his name* (as Saviour), *he gave power to become children of God; who were born, not of blood, nor of the will of the flesh, nor of the will of man, but of God.'* (John 1:12,13)

(iii) <u>Be baptized</u>

We must be baptized in the name of Jesus, to show God and the world our decision to begin a new life with Jesus Christ as our Saviour and Lord. *'You were buried with* [Christ] *in baptism, in which you were also raised with him through faith in the working of God...'* (Colossians 2:12) *"He who believes and is baptized will be saved..."* (Mark 16:16) *"Unless one is born of water and the Spirit, he cannot enter the Kingdom of God."* (John 3:5)

When we fulfil these three conditions, God promises us new life now and resurrection from the dead hereafter. *"We were buried therefore with him by baptism into death, so that as Christ was raised from the dead by the glory of the Father, we too might walk in newness of life. For if we have been united with him in a death like his, we shall certainly be united with him in a resurrection like his."* (Romans 6:4,5)

This rebirth is effected by the Holy Spirit. '*He saved us, not because of deeds done by us in righteousness, but in virtue of his own mercy, by the washing of regeneration and renewal in the Holy Spirit...*' (Titus 3:5)

New birth is not merely a figure of speech. When we are born again, something real happens to us. When I was born again, I was immediately filled with a sense of peace; I had a new love for other people, and the hymns I had sung since childhood suddenly made sense to me. Some people have a hunger to read the Bible. One young man I knew shut himself in his bedroom for three days to read it non-stop. Other people see the sky, trees, grass and flowers in brighter colours, as though nature itself has been through a washing machine.

But all this raises an important question. The Bible is clear that new birth involves baptism in the name of Jesus, and baptism means immersion in water, so does that mean that Christians who have never been immersed in water in the name of Jesus have not been born again? For example, I imagine that my hero, John Wesley, was only sprinkled with water as a baby, yet I am sure he was a born-again child of God. I believe the explanation is that God pardons genuine ignorance. James wrote, '*Whoever knows what is right to do and fails to do it, for him it is sin.*' (James 4:17)

God can do anything. He can bring us to life spiritually even if we haven't been baptized, so long as we have never understood his commandment to be baptized in the Biblical way. For example, in Acts 10 the Roman centurion Cornelius and his household received the Holy Spirit while Peter was still telling them about Jesus: they began speaking in tongues and extolling God. But as soon as Peter realized what had happened, he commanded them to be baptized in order to restore the situation in accordance with Jesus's instructions. I was brought up in a church which regarded the christening of infants as baptism, and when I was born again, I had not been baptized in the Biblical sense. I didn't even understand why Jesus had to die, but I certainly repented of my sin and unbelief, I committed my life to serving God as my creator, and my life did change as a result. The other things, including baptism, came later as God revealed them to me through his Word.

A more important question involves continuing sin. Can a child of God continue to live in sin? Can we be born again and continue to disobey God's laws and resist his will as Jesus has revealed it? And what happens if we do?

The Bible teaches us that when we are born of God, he sets us free from slavery to sin so that we can be free from it.

> *'Truly, truly, I say to you, every one who commits sin is a slave to sin. The slave does not continue in the house for ever; the son (anyone born of God) continues for ever. So if the Son makes you free, you will be free indeed.'* John 8:34-36

> *We know that our old self was crucified with him so that the sinful body might be destroyed, and we might no longer be enslaved to sin. For he who has died is freed from sin.* Romans 6:6,7

Some passages seem to go further, suggesting it's no longer possible to sin. *'No one born of God commits sin; for God's nature abides in him, and he cannot sin because he is born of God.'* (1 John 3:9) What did John mean by 'cannot'? Paul used the same word 'cannot' in 1 Corinthians 10:21: *'You cannot drink the cup of the Lord and the cup of demons.'* Evidently Paul didn't mean it was impossible to do both, because some of his church members were apparently doing this very thing. He meant that they absolutely mustn't do it; it was unthinkable for someone who believed in Jesus to have fellowship with both Jesus and demons. As children of God, we have been set free from slavery to sin and its hold over us, so how can we go back to a life of rebellion and disobedience from which Christ rescued us at the cost of his physical death? We have died to sin: to continue living in it is unthinkable. Worse than that, to go on sinning deliberately after accepting Christ as Saviour and Lord will not only incur severe punishment but will eventually lead to final destruction – the loss of our salvation. Read Hebrews 10:26-31 and 1 Corinthians 6:9,10.

Although we have been set free from slavery to sin, remaining free from it in all its forms is usually easier said than done. When I was about seven years old, my Sunday School teacher awarded me a decorated Bible verse to hang on my bedroom wall. It said, "Watch and pray, lest ye enter into temptation!" The price of freedom is eternal vigilance. The day we are born again, we enter into warfare with the world, the flesh and the devil. Some battles will indeed be won immediately. Others may continue, even for years. Long-standing addictions to drink, drugs, eating disorders, gambling, pornography, ungodly sexual attraction, etc., may or may not come to an end the day we are born again. The difference is that as God's children we can win every battle with the help of the Holy Spirit! (2 Corinthians 2:14; Philippians 4:13) Paul prayed three times for a particular thorn in the flesh to leave him, but in the end he had to learn to live with it. It was a constant reminder of his need to rely on the Lord and the strength of his might. (2 Corinthians 12:9; Ephesians 6:10)

To live fully as God's sons and daughters, we need three things:

(i) Power to overcome temptation

The world, the flesh and the devil are constantly trying to lead us back into sin, and in ourselves we don't have the strength to overcome them. Adam too was created a sinless son of God (Luke 3:38), but he fell into sin. The same thing will happen to us without special help.

(ii) Power to know God's will

It is one thing to want to do God's will, another always to know what it is. Jesus said, *"I always do what is pleasing to him."* (John 8:29) How did he always know what was pleasing to God? The Bible tells us the answer in general, but sometimes we face important decisions for which we need special guidance and direction.

(iii) <u>Power to do God's will</u>

Jesus said, *"Truly, truly, I say to you, he who believes in me will also do the works that I do."* (John 14:12) To do the things Jesus did, we certainly need supernatural power!

'*As he is, so are we in this world.*' (1 John 4:17) Many of us who have accepted Christ as Saviour and Lord have a genuine desire to serve him, yet we are not always overcoming the evil one, we are sometimes uncertain about God's will for us, and above all we feel powerless to help people like Jesus did. Our lives are characterized by struggle rather than victory, trial and error rather than clear guidance, impotence and frustration rather than power to turn the world upside down. We are not living in this world as Jesus did. We need something more.

Chapter 3: He enables us to live as Jesus lived on earth.

Water baptism

To be born again as children of God, we must repent of our sins and be immersed in water, either in the name of Jesus or in the name of the Father, Son and Holy Spirit. (John 3:3-5; Luke 24:47; Matthew 28:19; Acts 2:38)

The purpose of water baptism is to demonstrate publicly our repentance from sin, to confess our faith in Jesus as Saviour, and to prove our intention to live henceforth in obedience to him as Lord. Baptism signifies our decision to put our self-centred and sinful nature to death and to begin a new Christ-centred, holy life. It is the spiritual equivalent of a marriage service.

> *We were buried therefore with him by baptism into death, so that as Christ was raised from the dead by the glory of the Father, we too might walk in newness of life... our old self was crucified with him so that the sinful body might be destroyed, and we might no longer be enslaved to sin.*
>
> Romans 6:4,6

When we are baptized like this, God forgives our sin, brings our spirits to life in a new birth, and sets us free from sin's hold over us so that we can live in accordance with his will.

The New Covenant

That last point is really, really important. Jesus shed his blood on the cross to establish a new relationship between us and God, a relationship which God had promised through his prophets:

> *"But this is the covenant which I will make with the house of Israel after those days, says the Lord: I will put my law within them, and I will write it upon their hearts... I will forgive their iniquity, and I will remember their sin no more."*   Jeremiah 31:33

> *"I will sprinkle clean water upon you, and you shall be clean from all your uncleannesses, and from all your idols I will cleanse you. A new heart I will give you, and a new spirit I will put within you; and I will take out of your flesh the heart of stone and give you a heart of flesh. And I will put my spirit within you, and cause you to walk in my statutes and be careful to observe my ordinances..."*   Ezekiel 36:26,27

> *And he took a cup, and when he had given thanks he gave it to them, saying, "Drink of it, all of you; for this is my blood of the (new) covenant, which is poured out for many for the forgiveness of sins."*   Matthew 26:27,28

The Old Covenant was sealed with the blood of an ox. Some of the blood was sprinkled on the altar of burnt offering, and the rest upon representatives of the people. (Exodus 24:5-8) Blood was always understood to carry the life of an animal within it (Leviticus 17:11), so in this symbolical way God and his people came to share in a common life. At the Last Supper, Jesus handed the cup of wine to his disciples, saying it was his blood of the New Covenant. By drinking it, they could symbolically take his blood upon themselves and thus become partakers of the promised New Covenant. (1 Corinthians 10:16) Jesus confirmed God's commitment to the covenant when his actual blood was poured out on the cross.

In the New Covenant, as prophesied by Jeremiah and Ezekiel, God made five amazing promises to all of us who commit our lives to Jesus as Lord and Saviour:

(i) he gives us a new mind to know what his will is
(ii) he gives us a new spirit so that we want to do his will instead of rebelling against it
(iii) he forgives our past sins
(iv) he frees us from present sins
(v) he puts his Spirit within us.

Ezekiel distinguished between item (ii) God giving us a new spirit, and (v) God putting his Spirit within us. The first is new birth. The second is being filled with the Spirit, also termed 'baptism in the Holy Spirit' or simply 'receiving the Spirit.'

Receiving the Holy Spirit

In Mark 16:16 Jesus says, *"He who believes and is baptized will be saved,"* but Acts 19:1-6 shows us that being filled with the Spirit is something extra. St Paul had met some disciples at Ephesus and asked them if they had received the Holy Spirit when they believed. Discovering they had not even been baptized in the name of the Lord Jesus, he arranged for them to be baptized. According to Jesus, they were now baptized believers and therefore saved, but so far as Paul was concerned, that wasn't enough. Following their baptism, *'when Paul had laid his hands upon them, the Holy Spirit came on them; and they spoke with tongues and prophesied.'* So now these twelve new Christians had received the Holy Spirit when they believed.

The reason spiritual rebirth and being filled with the Spirit are often thought to be one and the same is because St Paul was convinced that everyone who is reborn by the Spirit of God should also be filled with the Spirit of God.

> *But you are not in the flesh, you are in the Spirit, if in fact the Spirit of God dwells in you. Anyone who does not have the Spirit of Christ does not belong to him. But if Christ is in you, although your bodies are dead because of sin, your spirits are alive because of righteousness. If the Spirit of him who raised Jesus from the dead dwells in you, he who raised Christ Jesus from the dead will give life to your mortal bodies also through his Spirit which dwells in you.* Romans 8:9-11

Paul uses several words and phrases to describe the Spirit of God, but what he is saying is that the Spirit of God dwells in everyone who has been brought to life spiritually, or he should do, because that is what Jesus promised. *'I will pray the Father, and he will give you another Counselor, to be with you for ever, even the Spirit of truth... he dwells with you, and will be in you."* (John 14:16,17)

The Bible teaches us that when we are filled with God's Spirit we can speak and act with supernatural abilities. We can do the kinds of things Jesus did, things that he promised those who believed in him would be able to do. (John 14:12) The Bible shows this in a host of different ways.

In the life of Jesus

God told John the Baptist that the promised Messiah was about to come, and he told John how to recognize him. Here's what John testified: *"...he who sent me to baptize with water said to me, 'He on whom you see the Spirit descend and remain, this is he who baptizes with the Holy Spirit.'"* (John 1:33)

Luke describes how this happened. *'Now when all the people were baptized, and when Jesus also had been baptized and was praying, the heaven was opened, and <u>the Holy Spirit descended upon him</u> in bodily form as a dove,* *and a voice came from heaven, "Thou art my beloved Son; with thee I am well pleased."*(Luke 3:21,22) Later St Peter said, *"God <u>anointed</u> Jesus of Nazareth with the Holy Spirit and with power."* (Acts 10:38)

Jesus was already born of the Spirit, and he was already the Son of God (Luke 1:35), yet it wasn't until his baptism that the Holy Spirit descended upon him and anointed him with power. Until that moment he hadn't preached or worked any miracles, even though he was the Son of God. (Luke 3:23; John 2:11) He had to be 'anointed with the Holy Spirit and power' in order to carry out his mission and ministry. Luke describes the results: 'And Jesus, <u>*full of the Holy Spirit*</u>, *returned from the Jordan...*' (Luke 4:1) Filled with the Holy Spirit and power, Jesus could now deal with Satan and his temptations; he knew what God had called him to do and how he was to do it; and he began his ministry of preaching, healing and deliverance from demonic powers and bondages.

- Jesus could now deal effectively with the devil. '*And Jesus, <u>full of the Holy Spirit</u>, returned from the Jordan, and was led by the Spirit for forty days in the wilderness, tempted by the devil... And Jesus answered him, "It is said, 'You shall not tempt the Lord your God.'" And when the devil had ended every temptation, he departed from him until an opportune time.*' (Luke 4:1,12,13)
- Jesus now knew what he had to do and how to do it. He spoke and acted with authority and confidence. '*And Jesus returned <u>in the power of the Spirit</u> into Galilee, and a report concerning him went out through all the surrounding country. And he taught in their synagogues, being glorified by all... He opened the book and found the place where it was written, "<u>The Spirit of the Lord is upon me</u>, because <u>he has anointed me</u> to preach good news to the poor. He has sent me to proclaim release to the captives and recovering of sight to the blind, to set at liberty those who are oppressed, to proclaim the acceptable year of the Lord."* (Luke 4:14,15,17-19)

- He had power to cast out demons and heal the sick. *'And in the synagogue there was a man who had the spirit of an unclean demon; and he cried out with a loud voice, "Ah! What have you to do with us, Jesus of Nazareth? Have you come to destroy us? I know who you are, the Holy One of God." But Jesus rebuked him, saying, "Be silent, and come out of him!" And when the demon had thrown him down in the midst, he came out of him, having done him no harm. And they were all amazed and said to one another, "What is this word? For <u>with authority and power</u> he commands the unclean spirits, and they come out." ...Now when the sun was setting, all those who had any that were sick with various diseases brought them to him; and he laid his hands on every one of them and healed them.'* (Luke 4:33-36,40)

The underlined phrases all refer to the same experience: 'the Spirit descended on Jesus and remained', 'God anointed him with the Holy Spirit and with power', he was then 'full of the Holy Spirit', and he returned from the wilderness 'in the power of the Spirit' because 'the Spirit of the Lord was upon him.'

Jesus was born of God all his life. But being anointed by the Holy Spirit, being filled with the Holy Spirit, being in the power of the Holy Spirit – this was something separate, something extra, something that first happened at his baptism. And without this additional power, even Jesus could never have accomplished his mission. That is because, Paul said, that when Jesus came to the earth, he left behind all the abilities only God could have in order to become just like us.

Though he was in the form of God [he] *did not count equality with God a thing to be grasped, but emptied himself, taking the form of a servant, being born in the likeness of men.* Philippians 2:6.7

It's easy to assume that because Jesus was the Son of God, he had supernatural powers from birth. But that kind of thinking leads to the conviction that we can never be like Jesus. The whole point of Jesus's incarnation was to become like us, to show us how we can live if sin is eradicated from our lives. As the ancient Bishop Irenaeus said, 'He became what we are in order that we might become what he is.' It was not because Jesus was the Son of God that he was able to accomplish his amazing ministry: it was because he was anointed by the Spirit at his baptism. *"It is by the Spirit of God that I cast out demons,"* he said. (Matthew 12:28)

Astonishingly, God wants you and me as believers to be just like Jesus, and to do the kinds of thing Jesus did. *"As the Father has sent me, even so I send you,"* he told his first disciples. 'He who says he abides in him ought to walk in the same way in which he walked.' 'As he is, so are we in this world.' *"He who believes in me will also do the works that I do."* The words 'he who believes in me' mean that this applies to every disciple. (John 14.12; 1 John 2:6; 4:17; John 20:21)

To emulate Jesus as God wants us to, we must *first* be born of the Holy Spirit and *then* we must be filled with the Holy Spirit as he was.

In the lives of the first Christians

It is this second step of being filled with the Spirit which so often is missing in our lives today. 'And [Paul] *said to them, "Did you receive the Holy Spirit when you believed?" And they said, "No, we have never even heard that there is a Holy Spirit."* (Acts 19.2)

Let's see how God filled some of the first Christians with the Holy Spirit, and the various ways in which this experience is described.

(i) The apostles

And while staying with them [Jesus] *charged them not to depart from Jerusalem, but to wait for the promise of the Father, which, he said, "you heard from me, for John baptized with water, but before many days you shall be baptized with* (immersed in) *the Holy Spirit."*   Acts 1:4,5

"But you shall receive power when the Holy Spirit has come upon you, and you shall be my witnesses..."   Acts 1:8

When the day of Pentecost had come, they were all together in one place. And suddenly a sound came from heaven like the rush of a mighty wind, and it filled all the house where they were sitting. And there appeared to them tongues as of fire, distributed and resting on each of them. And they were all filled with the Holy Spirit, and began to speak in other tongues, as the Spirit gave them utterance.   Acts 2:1-4

(ii) <u>The Gentile centurion Cornelius and his household</u>

While Peter was still saying this, the Holy Spirit fell on all who heard the word. And the believers... who came with Peter were amazed, because the gift of the Holy Spirit had been poured out even on the Gentiles. For they heard them speaking in tongues and extolling God. Then Peter declared, "Can anyone forbid water for baptizing these people who have received the Holy Spirit just as we have?"   Acts 10:44-47

(iii) <u>Twelve disciples at Ephesus</u>

On hearing this, they were baptized in the name of the Lord Jesus. And when Paul had laid his hands upon them, the Holy Spirit came on them; and they spoke with tongues and prophesied.   Acts 19:5,6

(iv) <u>Various people</u>

Then Peter, filled with the Holy Spirit, said to them...   Acts 4:8

And when they had prayed, the place in which they were gathered together was shaken; and they were all filled with the Holy Spirit and spoke the word of God with boldness.' Acts 4:31

...and they chose Stephen, a man full of faith and of the Holy Spirit... Acts 6:5

"Brother Saul, the Lord Jesus who appeared to you on the road by which you came, has sent me that you may regain your sight and be filled with the Holy Spirit." Acts 9:17

But Saul, who is also called Paul, filled with the Holy Spirit, looked intently at him and said, "You son of the devil..." Acts 13:9,10

And the disciples were filled with joy and with the Holy Spirit. Acts 13:52

It appears that the book of Acts is trying to tell us something about being filled with the Holy Spirit! It is indisputable that these verses are not about being born again. No one can be born again more than once, but they tell us that Peter was filled with the Holy Spirit on at least three separate occasions and Paul on at least two. Being filled with the Holy Spirit is a separate experience to the new birth: these passages cannot be explained in any other way.

The book of Acts clearly teaches us that being filled with the Spirit can occur more than once; and that when it happens, it enables believers to speak in other languages, to speak the word of God with boldness and wisdom, to extol God, to work wonders and signs, or to discern what is in men's hearts. That's why Paul urged the born-again believers in Ephesus, *'Be filled with the Holy Spirit.'* (Ephesians 5:18) If that was the same thing as being born again, he'd have been telling them to be born again again! The Greek literally means, 'keep on being filled with the

Holy Spirit', and that is what he wants you and me to do. Being filled with the Spirit is a choice: it has to be our choice as well as God's.

In the lives of Old Testament characters

Another way to understand the difference between new birth and being filled with the Spirit is to read how God sometimes filled people who were *not* born again with his Spirit! No one could be born again until Jesus had died. The New Covenant, in which God promised to give his people a new heart and a new spirit, was not instituted until Jesus had died as *'the Lamb of God who takes away the sins of the world.'* So even John the Baptist was not born again. Jesus told his disciples, "*Among those born of women none is greater than John; yet he who is least in the kingdom of God is greater than he.*" (Luke 7:28) John had not entered the kingdom of God when he died because he had been born only of women, not of God, yet he was *'filled with the Holy Spirit, even from his mother's womb.'* (Luke 1:15) That was how he was able to have such a powerful ministry. Of course, I am not suggesting that John won't have a place in God's coming kingdom. He would be among the Old Testament prophets and men and women of God whom Jesus rescued from Hades between Good Friday and Easter Sunday. (1 Peter 3:18-20; 4:6; Ephesians 4:8)

Consider the following examples of Old Testament characters who were either permanently or temporarily filled with the Holy Spirit. They were not born again under the New Covenant, and some of them were not even very godly, yet they were undeniably Spirit-filled people!

The Lord said to Moses, "See, I have called by name Bezalel the son of Uri, son of Hur, of the tribe of Judah; and I have filled him with the Spirit of God, with ability and intelligence, with knowledge and all craftsmanship, to devise artistic designs, to work in gold, silver, and bronze, in cutting stones for setting, and in carving wood, for work in every craft.

Exodus 31:1-5

...And behold, a young lion roared against [Samson]; *and the Spirit of the Lord came mightily upon him, and he tore the lion asunder as one tears a kid; and he had nothing in his hand.* Judges 14:5,6

And Saul went from there to Naioth in Ramah; and the Spirit of God came upon him also, and as he went he prophesied, until he came to Naioth in Ramah. 1 Samuel 19:23

The Spirit of the Lord God is upon me, because the Lord has anointed me to bring good tidings to the afflicted... Isaiah 61:1

Then Samuel took the horn of oil, and anointed [David] *in the midst of his brothers; and the Spirit of the Lord came mightily upon David from that day forward.* 1 Samuel 16:13

One exciting lesson from the above is that the Holy Spirit can enable us to do supernaturally well all kinds of different things God might want us to do. It could be to make jewellery or to be supernaturally brave and strong; to prophesy and preach; or to rule a kingdom. It could be to heal the sick or cast out demons. It could be almost any activity that promotes the kingdom of God. Hopefully, the Holy Spirit has even enabled me to write a useful book!

Conclusion

To be brought to life spiritually and to enter the kingdom of God we must be born again as sons and daughters of God by repentance and baptism into the life of Jesus. In this way we publicly show our faith in Jesus as Saviour and our desire to obey him as Lord and live as genuine citizens of his kingdom.

Next, to fulfil whatever ministry God has given us, and in particular to fulfil Christ's promise that as believers we will have power to do the kinds of things he did, we must be anointed by, or filled with, God's Spirit. That is something distinct from the new birth, and it may have to take place more than once.

St Paul summarized this teaching in Galatians. '*For as many of you as were baptized into Christ have put on Christ... Because you are sons, God has sent the Spirit of his Son into our hearts...*' (Galatians 3:27; 4:6)

So let's see how God does this, and what happens when he does...

Chapter 4: How can I receive the Holy Spirit?

The promise of the Spirit

"If any one hears my voice and opens the door, I will come in to him and eat with him, and he with me." (Revelation 3:20) Jesus made this promise to Christians in the church of Laodicea. This is the promise of the Spirit, the 'other Counsellor', for those of us who recognize and admit our need of his help. *"I will pray the Father, and he will give you another Counsellor, to be with you for ever, even the Spirit of truth, whom the world cannot receive, because it neither sees him nor knows him; you know him, for he dwells with you, and will be in you."* (John 14:17) Since the world cannot receive the Spirit of Christ, this promise is obviously made to those who are already Christians.

Sometimes, believers drawing near to God have been powerfully filled with the Spirit without specifically asking him to do this. Such people often seem to have been special men and women of God whom he has greatly used, like the evangelists D. L. Moody and Charles Finney. Nevertheless, Jesus promised that the heavenly Father will give the Holy Spirit to any of his children who ask him to.

> *"Every one who asks receives, and he who seeks finds, and to him who knocks it will be opened. What father among you, if his son asks for a fish, will instead of a fish give him a serpent; or if he asks for an egg, will give him a scorpion? If you then, who are evil, know how to give good gifts to your children, how much more will the heavenly Father give the Holy Spirit to those who ask him!"*   Luke 11:13

Therefore, if God is your heavenly Father, if you have become one of his children by being born again in the way I have described earlier, the promise is for you as well!

However, there do seem to be some conditions for God to fulfil this promise.

Admit your need.

How can we receive something if we believe we have it already? In his book, *The Christian Warfare*, Dr Martyn Lloyd-Jones wrote:

> "[You say] *it happened when I was born again, at my conversion; there is nothing for me to seek, I have got it all."* Got it all? Well, if you have *"got it all",* I simply ask in the Name of God, why are you as you are? If you have *"got it all"...* why are you so unlike the New Testament Christians?... You cannot be baptized or filled with the Holy Spirit without knowing it. It is the greatest experience one can ever know.

"Blessed are the poor in spirit, for theirs is the kingdom of heaven." (Matthew 5:3) Only those who know they are spiritually poor can be made rich. Jesus condemned the church at Laodicea, not for being needy, but for not admitting her need: *"For you say, I am rich, I have prospered, and I need nothing: not knowing that you are wretched, pitiable, poor, blind and naked."* (Revelation 3:17) But then he said, *"If any one hears my voice and opens the door, I will come in..."* In other words, if they would acknowledge their need of help, he would come into each one of them in the person of the Holy Spirit to restore them to a life of holiness, faith and love.

As I mentioned in the Introduction, the Holy Spirit showed me my own need of him as I was reading Galatians 5:22,23: *'The fruit of the Spirit is love, joy, peace, patience, kindness, goodness, faithfulness, gentleness, self-control.'* My lack of *all* this fruit convinced me that I needed to pray for the Holy Spirit.

There has to come a point at which we discover we cannot live as God wants us to, or do any of the things he wants us to do, without the indwelling presence of his Spirit in our life.

Believe the promise.

In his letter to the Galatian church, chapter 3 and verse 2, Paul asked them, *'Did you receive the Spirit by works of the law, or by hearing with faith?'* This shows that the Spirit is given, not as a reward for good behaviour, but as a gift to those who have complete faith in God's promise.

I was a young Methodist minister when some people prayed for me to be filled with the Holy Spirit. At the time nothing spectacular seemed to happen, only a great stillness as though I no longer needed to ask any further. In some ways I felt disappointed, but those praying for me assured me that God had answered their prayers, which was some encouragement. I decided I would hold fast to God's promise to give his Spirit to me if I asked, and that since I had asked, I would believe he had done so, whether or not there was any immediate evidence. And some evidence did come the very next day.

One reason I had wanted to be filled with the Spirit was to be able to talk to people I met about the Lord. Early next morning as I was walking my small son in his pushchair in the local park, I found myself, with no deliberate effort, talking about the Lord to a park keeper. This was so encouraging!

A few weeks later a lady from one of my congregations wrote a letter to me saying how blessed she had been in the previous Sunday's service I led. She said my sermon was so much more full of life than the one I had preached on my first visit there!

Peter said, *"The promise is to you and to your children and to all that are far off, every one whom the Lord our God calls to him."* (Acts 2:39) Read God's Word on this subject until you believe that the promise really is for you!

Desire the gift.

The evangelist R. A. Torrey said that an intense desire to be filled with the Spirit is an essential requirement for God to do this. A. W. Tozer agreed, in his book *How to be filled with the Holy Spirit*.

God fills us with his Spirit so that we can glorify Jesus by becoming channels of his truth, love and saving power to lost sinners. Jesus said, *"He will glorify me, for he will take what is mine and declare it to you."* (John 16:14) The word translated 'declare' can mean 'to pass on.' Jesus was saying that the Holy Spirit would pass on to us all we require to seek and save lost sinners in the same way that he did. If we genuinely want to glorify Jesus by continuing his work of salvation, we must genuinely desire to be filled with his Spirit, for he said, *"Apart from me you can do nothing."* (John 15:5)

Jesus told two stories about people who kept on asking for help: a widow who unceasingly pestered a judge for justice, and a man who kept banging on his neighbour's door at night until the disgruntled neighbour got out of bed to lend him three loaves for an unexpected visitor. We usually conclude that Jesus was teaching us to keep on asking God for something we need, but I think his key point was that these two people got what they asked for because they wanted it so desperately. It was the widow's intense desire for justice and the man's intense desire for some food that would not allow them to give up. Paul told the Corinthians to '*earnestly desire the spiritual gifts*', and the number one gift of the Holy Spirit is himself!

Soon after the Lord filled my wife and me with the Spirit, my brother-in-law travelled 200 miles to meet us, firmly believing God would fill him with his Spirit when we prayed for him. He did! My sister was seven and a half months pregnant with their first child, and her doctor had sternly advised her against travelling so far, so we prayed for her at a distance. As we did so, my brother-in-law started to speak in tongues. He was so excited!

Back home he prayed for my sister to be filled with the Spirit too, but she only burst into tears. For three days she continued to seek the Lord about this, and finally God was able to answer her prayers.

"I realized that the past few days, which could have been a time of complete despair, had in fact been a time for peace and confidence," she wrote. "I suddenly experienced a feeling of tremendous joy that the Holy Spirit, the Comforter, had indeed been with me... I had this very gentle experience of warmth and peace, which I knew was the Holy Spirit coming into my life... I had crossed the threshold into the life of the Spirit."

Do you earnestly and wholeheartedly desire to have this life-changing gift from God, so much so that you will let nothing stand in the way of receiving it?

Surrender.

'Do you not know that your body is a temple of the Holy Spirit within you, which you have from God? You are not your own; you were bought with a price. So glorify God in your body.' (1 Corinthians 6:19,20)

We were slaves to sin until the day when Jesus bought our freedom at the cost of his own life and brought us into the family of God. So although our heavenly Father doesn't treat us as slaves but as sons and daughters, there is a sense in which even our bodies now belong to him. *'I appeal to you therefore brethren, by the mercies of God, to present your bodies as a living sacrifice, holy and acceptable to God, which is your spiritual worship.'* (Romans 12:1) When God's Spirit takes up residence in our bodies, we must offer him the use of our heart, mind, will, hands, feet and tongue. In that way the Spirit can manifest God's presence, holiness, love and power through us.

Be willing to surrender yourself completely to the Holy Spirit. Don't be afraid of making such a surrender. Fear comes from Satan, not from God. God is love, and his Spirit can only bring good to us. Yield every part of your being to the Holy Spirit and let him do whatever he wants to do with you and through you.

Seek help.

Jesus assured us that our heavenly Father will give us the Holy Spirit if we ask, but in the New Testament there isn't a single instance of someone receiving the Spirit on their own. It's not impossible – that's what happened to my wife, as well as to those evangelists I mentioned – but in the early church they usually prayed for each other to receive the promise of the Father. (Acts 8:14-17; 9:17; 19:6; 2 Timothy 1:6,7) Moreover, it was always when believers were together, seeking to be in the centre of God's will, that the Spirit was poured out upon them in power. (Acts 2:1-4; 4:31; 10:44) It quickly became the practice to pray for a new believer to be filled with the Spirit when he emerged from the waters of baptism.

It may be humbling to ask others to pray for you, particularly if you are a leader in the church, but God's Word says, *'Humble yourselves before the Lord, and he will exalt you.'* (James 4:10) Let Christ's people share in your search, and share in your joy of finding!

Ask God.

Once you are convinced of your need to be filled with the Holy Spirit, once you believe God is willing to do this, and once you sincerely desire him to fill you with his Spirit, then you should ask him to do so, preferably with the help of your church leaders or Christian friends. Perhaps one or two of them will pray for you, laying their hands on you in the name of Jesus. (Hebrews 6:2) Your part is to look to your heavenly Father, believing he will give you what he has promised. *"Therefore I tell you, whatever you ask in prayer, believe that you have received it, and it will be yours."* (Mark 11:24)

Keep asking.

It is possible God will not grant your request immediately. At his ascension, Jesus told his disciples to wait in Jerusalem for the promise of the Father. They had to continue in prayer for another nine days until the Holy Spirit fell on them in a rushing wind and with visible tongues of fire. Spiritual revivals are almost always preceded by long periods of increasingly earnest prayer, usually accompanied by deep repentance from sin. God's timing is important. Sometimes there may be things that still have to be cleared out of you before your house is ready for such a heavenly guest. If that is so God, will show you.

The important thing is not to give up. Don't allow the devil to suggest that the gift of the Spirit is not for you: it is for *'everyone whom the Lord our God calls to him.'* (Acts 2:39) Don't let the devil put you off with thoughts that you are not worthy to receive such a gift. No one is! Jesus told the parable of the unrighteous judge *'to the effect that they ought always to pray and not lose heart.'* (Luke 18: 1) And he concluded: *"Will not God vindicate his elect, who cry to him day and night? Will he delay long over them? I tell you, he will vindicate them speedily."* (Luke 18:7,8) So *'continue steadfastly in prayer'* (Colossians 4:2) and the Lord will keep his promise to you!

What will happen?

At one extreme you may feel as though you are on fire and burst out in torrents of praise, either in your own language or one the Spirit gives you; conversely, you may feel very little except a deep sense of peace. You may find yourself breathing in deeply, perhaps almost gasping for breath; or you may feel so enfolded in God's love that you burst into tears. Some people collapse on the floor in a state of semi-consciousness; others are so filled with joy that they can't stop laughing. The important thing is to surrender yourself completely to God, allowing him to meet you in whatever manner he chooses.

Praise God.

If you believe God has kept his promise, thanksgiving and praise will be your natural reaction. The Bible shows that the first thing people do when the Spirit first comes upon them is to praise God.

> We hear them telling in our own tongues the mighty works of God.
> Acts 2:11

> While Peter was still saying this, the Holy Spirit fell on all who heard the word. And the believers... were amazed, because the gift of the Holy Spirit had been poured out even on the Gentiles. For they heard them speaking in tongues and extolling God.
> Acts 10:44-46

So speak out! Praise God for his greatness and his love. Thank him for his gift. Focus on God rather than yourself and let the Holy Spirit give you the words. (Romans 8:15,16)

Give the Holy Spirit control.

If you are not already speaking in a language the Spirit gives you, stop thinking altogether about the words you are using. Give the Holy Spirit complete control of your tongue. Why is this important? It's because what we say, think and do are intimately linked together. While it is hard to allow the Holy Spirit to control what we think and do, we *can* give him control of what we say. When we do that, he can control what we think and feel and do as well.

> Look at the ships also; though they are so great and are driven by strong winds, they are guided by a very small rudder wherever the will of the pilot directs. So the tongue is a little member and boasts of great things.

James 3:4,5

When the captain of a ship hands control of the rudder to the pilot, he is giving him control of the entire ship. When we give our tongue to the Holy Spirit, we are giving him control of everything else in us. It is a practical way by which we can surrender ourselves completely to him.

I appeal to you therefore, brethren, by the mercies of God, to present your bodies as a living sacrifice, holy and acceptable to God, which is your spiritual worship. Romans 12:1

In the Bible, when Christians were filled with the Spirit, they spoke in words given by the Holy Spirit in languages which they themselves did not themselves understand.

And they were all filled with the Holy Spirit and began to speak in other tongues (languages), *as the Spirit gave them utterance... And* [the multitude] *were amazed and wondered, saying, "Are not all these who are speaking Galileans? And how is it that we hear, each of us in his own native language?... We hear them telling in our own tongues the mighty works of God.* Acts 2:4-11

Notice that the *disciples* spoke, the *Spirit* gave them the words. This means that *we* have to do the speaking by opening our mouth and starting to speak, but the *Spirit* gives us the words to express what is in our hearts. He does not 'possess' us as an evil spirit might possess a person. We don't go into a trance nor lose consciousness. We can speak quickly or slowly, loudly or quietly, and stop or start as we wish. We do the speaking: the Spirit gives us the words. And the words he gives will express the deepest desires and thoughts and feelings of our hearts. (Romans 8:26,27) The language of the Spirit is a language of trust and love. "*Daddy! Father!*" (Galatians 4:6) It is direct communication between our spirit and God, without the limitations imposed by our human mind. (1 Corinthians 14:2,14) It is God's gift for building us up in holiness, faith and love. (1 Corinthians 14:4a)

Although Paul says that when we pray in tongues our minds remain unfruitful, we should still keep them focussed on the Lord. Keep your mind on him, not on what you are saying, and certainly not on what you are going to have for dinner today! Whether you want to express your love or gratitude to Jesus, to intercede for someone or something for which you need the Spirit's help, or you just want to pour out your deepest feelings to an understanding heavenly Father, keep your mind firmly focussed on the One you are speaking to. You are not simply spouting a lot of words into thin air: you are addressing your creator!

Sometimes people find it hard to pray in tongues for the first time. The secret is to forget your fears and to trust completely in the Holy Spirit. It's rather like learning to swim. When I was learning to swim, I knew the water could support me because I had seen it support other people. I believed in my mind that it could support me, but there had to come a moment when I put my belief into practice. Despite my fears, I had to take my feet off the bottom of the pool and let the water take hold of me. In that moment I found I could swim!

Jesus said that those who believe in him would speak in new tongues. When the centurion Cornelius and his household burst out spontaneously in tongues of praise, Peter saw this as proof that God had accepted them as his children, even though they were not Jews. So speaking in tongues can help to assure us that God has heard our prayer for his Spirit to dwell within us. The devil, as usual, will try to rob us of God's gift by telling us it isn't of God. Don't believe the devil. Believe the Lord Jesus! Once again, he said:

> "What father among you, if his son asks for a fish, will instead of a fish give him a serpent; or if he asks for an egg, will give him a scorpion? If you

then, who are evil, know how to give good gifts to your children, how much more will the heavenly Father give the Holy Spirit to those who ask him?"
Luke 11:11-13

You may say only a couple of words to start with. But that's how babies learn to talk. Press on, day by day, and you will grow more and more fluent.

The two pastors who prayed for me to receive the Holy Spirit did not themselves speak in tongues, and perhaps because of that I didn't either. But I did believe God had answered their prayers for me and my life did change. For one thing, I had a new love for him, and before long I wanted to express this love more fully with words that the Spirit gave me. Endlessly repeating, "I love you, God," seemed inadequate. So I tried a couple of times to speak in tongues by faith, but each time I quickly came to a halt, convinced that I was merely saying silly things in my own strength. (Later, after God called me and my wife to serve him in Chile and I started to learn Spanish, I discovered that a word I had repeated over and over again, *llena*, was the Spanish for 'fill'!)

Several weeks later, I tried a third time, and this time I pressed on by faith. As I continued to speak to the Lord, I began to sense his presence with me. It was a Sunday afternoon, shortly before I was due to set out and lead worship in a small Methodist chapel in the heart of Norfolk. I was the first to arrive, and once inside I said a brief prayer. After the service, the Chapel Steward and his wife came to me and said, "We knew it was going to be special today. As soon as we entered the chapel this afternoon, we could feel the presence of God."

Use the gift that you have in faith, and the difference it makes to your life will soon convince you it is of the Lord.

Sometimes the Spirit engulfs us in an extraordinary display of power. Here is Pastor Paul Martini's description of his encounter with the Spirit in 2014.

Heat that I had never felt before came over me like a vortex. I began to shake with what felt like electricity running through my body, while at the same time I would violently crunch my body as spasms of power hit me, all the while feeling tremendous heat... People around me said I was literally radiating heat...

I have seen tremendous growth in myself as a result of God's touch. I am able to hear the Lord and follow where He is leading in a meeting. My preaching and teaching have become more effective... I have seen deaf ears open up, people on life support with no hope come back to life, cancerous brain tumours disappear, and even the crippled start to walk. All of this brings more glory to Jesus Christ. I'm so grateful for all that God has done and continues to do.

From *Baptized in the Spirit* by Randy Clark

That is surely what Jesus was talking about when he told his first disciples, *"You shall receive power when the Holy Spirit comes upon you, and you shall be my witnesses..."*

It is possible, even in the 21st century!

Chapter 5: Overcoming evil

Called to be holy

There is no question that to live with the Lord in his coming kingdom, we must be holy people. *'Strive for the holiness without which no one will see the Lord,'* the writer of Hebrews tells us. (Hebrews 12:14)

As obedient children, do not be conformed to the passions of your former ignorance, but as he who called you is holy, be holy yourselves in all your conduct; since it is written, "You shall be holy, for I am holy."
1 Peter 1:14-16

But you are a chosen race, a royal priesthood, a holy nation, God's own people, that you may declare the wonderful deeds of him who called you out of darkness into his marvellous light. 1 Peter 2:9

To be holy is to be set apart from sin in order to serve the Lord. And for this to happen, we need the help of the Holy Spirit.

In Old Testament times, God gave his people laws which explained what they must do to live a holy life. However, they never managed to keep God's laws for long, because deeply embedded in all human nature there is a rebellion against God. It is a kind of spiritual disease which we have all inherited from Adam. And until this disease is cured, we cannot live as God wants us to, however hard we try. (Romans 7:13-24)

But there is an answer. *'Thanks be to God, [it's] through Jesus Christ our Lord!* (Romans 7:25) Because we cannot free ourselves from sin's hold over us, God in his love sent Jesus Christ to destroy the power of sin by his death, and to enable us to keep his laws and live a holy life with him forever.

> *For God has done what the law, weakened by the flesh, could not do; sending his own Son in the likeness of sinful flesh and for sin, he condemned sin in the flesh, in order that the just requirement of the law might be fulfilled in us, who walk not according to the flesh, but according to the Spirit.* Romans 8:3,4

God's plan is that we should be governed now, not by a set of written regulations, but by a person – the Holy Spirit.

> *But now we are discharged from the law, dead to that which held us captive, so that we serve not under the old written code, but in the new life of the Spirit.* Romans 7:6

Does that mean we no longer need the laws of the Old Testament? No! For often the Spirit will speak to us through the law. Since God gave the law, the Spirit of God will not tell us to do anything which contradicts it, so we need to know what the law says to be sure that it really is the Holy Spirit who is leading us.

Basically, the Spirit enables us to obey God in two ways.

First, through the rebirth of our spirit, he gives us a new nature. Born of the Holy Spirit, we are no longer rebellious children of the devil: we are now children of a holy God, and we share in his holy nature. So we no longer rebel against God's laws: we want to live as God wants us to. (John 1:12,13; Jeremiah 31:33; Ezekiel 36:27; 1 John 3:9)

Second, by coming himself to live within us and help us, the Spirit gives us power to overcome the temptations which come to everyone, and which came even to Jesus. (Hebrews 4:15)

So above all else the ministry of the Holy Spirit is to make us holy, to turn us into people who hate sin and love God, people who do the will of God not because we have to but because we want to, people who serve him not out of duty but out of love. The heart of God's promised New Covenant is that he will cleanse us from sin and from all its consequences.

How far has God fulfilled this promise in you?

Three kinds of churchgoer

Let's face it, there are three kinds of churchgoer for whom the promise of holiness has not yet been fulfilled.

Firstly, there are people who don't take sin seriously. They may attend church only for social reasons and perhaps are not even trying to be followers of Christ. Or it may be that their church doesn't teach them about the seriousness of sin.

The reason Jesus had to die was not to pay the penalty of our sin for us so that we may continue to live in sin: it was to break sin's hold over us so that we can live holy, righteous lives. Actually, the Bible never says that Christ paid the penalty for sin in our place. He certainly paid a price, an appalling price for our salvation, but the penalty for sin is the final and permanent death of both body and soul in hell. Thankfully, that is a penalty God did not ask his Son to pay for us!

What the Bible says is that Jesus 'bore our sins'. What that means is that he bore the *consequence* of our sins, in the sense of physical death. Ideally, people should bear the consequences of their own sins. For example, Leviticus 24:15,16 says, *'Whoever curses his God shall bear his sin. He who blasphemes the name of the Lord shall be put to death.'* But Jesus bore the consequence of *our* sins in the form of physical death, even though he had committed no sin himself.

Physical death is the most obvious consequence of sin, for Genesis tells us that if Adam and Eve had continued to obey God's commandments, they would have been able to live for ever. So when

Jesus died on the cross, he bore the physical consequence of our sins. Why did he do this? Peter tells us: *'He himself bore our sins in his body on the tree, that we might die to sin and live to righteousness.'* (1 Peter 2:24) In Peter's words, Jesus did not come to *pay* for our sins but to *set us free* from them. When we are set free from sin, there is no longer anything to keep us out of God's everlasting kingdom. Here's what Jesus himself said about it:

> *Jesus answered them, "Truly, truly, I say to you, every one who commits sin is a slave to sin. The slave does not continue in the house for ever; the son continues for ever. So if the Son makes you free, you will be free indeed."* John 8:34-36

It is fashionable to teach that if we believe Jesus has paid for our sins we shall be saved, even if we continue to commit them. But that is not at all what Jesus taught! He said, *"Not everyone who says to me, 'Lord, Lord,' shall enter the kingdom of heaven, but he who does the will of my Father who is in heaven."* (Matthew 7:21) He said that not even a prophetic or miraculous ministry carried out in his name will rescue us on the day of judgement, if we persist in sin.

> *"On that day many will say to me, 'Lord, Lord, did we not prophesy in your name, and cast out demons in your name, and do many mighty works in your name?' And then I will declare to them, 'I never knew you; depart from me, you evildoers.'"* Matthew 7:22,23

> *Little children, let no one deceive you. He who does right is righteous, as he is righteous. He who commits sin is of the devil; for the devil has sinned from the beginning. The reason the Son of God appeared was to destroy the works of the devil. No one born of God commits sin.* 1 John 3:7,8

In his mercy, God freely forgives the sins of those who truly repent of their sins and turn to Christ in order to live as God wants them to. But if as a believer in Christ you continue to swear or lie, if you continue to harbour jealous or unforgiving or hateful or lustful thoughts, if you continue to engage in dishonest or deceitful practices, if you are engaging in sexual activity with someone to whom you are not married, if you know you are not living as Jesus commanded you to; and if at the same time you are not grieving over your behaviour or earnestly seeking God's help to bring it all to an end, then *you have not repented*, and without repentance there is no forgiveness of sins! (Luke 13:3,5; 24:47)

Secondly, there are people who want to be free from sin, but for one reason or another they remain trapped in it. They may be involved in some obvious form of sexual immorality or another kind of sin, yet not totally want to give it up; or they may have become so addicted to drugs or alcohol or gluttony or gambling or pornography that they find it impossible to change their behaviour; or they may simply be trying to live as Jesus taught us to live, yet feel guilty because they know they are failing. This latter group may not be ruled by the Old Testament laws as devout Jews are, but in reality they have simply substituted Jesus's laws for the Old Testament ones. Consequently, they fail even more miserably because his laws are set to an even higher standard.

One possible explanation of all these conditions is that the people concerned have never been born again. The hold of sin over them has not been broken by God's supernatural revelation and intervention. The rebellion in their hearts has not been healed. For them, the motive to obey God has to come through an outward law, and this motive is not strong enough to overcome the rebelliousness of a sinful nature. Once again, through his prophet Ezekiel God gave this amazing promise of deliverance:

"A new heart I will give you, and a new spirit I will put within you; and I will take out of your flesh the heart of stone, and give you a heart of flesh.

And I will put my spirit within you, and cause you to walk in my statutes and be careful to observe my ordinances."   Ezekiel 36:26,27

New birth is a supernatural change that takes place when we truly repent of all our sins, when we believe that Jesus Christ can and will save us from sin's penalty and power, and when we fully commit our life to serve him as Lord. It has nothing to do with how good or bad we feel we are. It is a matter of putting ourselves into Christ's hands to do whatever he wants to do - with us, in us, and through us. If you think you need to be born again, read Chapter 2 once more and then, if you are sure you want to live 100% for Jesus for the rest of your life, whatever it costs, turn to the Epilogue and make the prayer of commitment there your own.

Thirdly, there are people who *have* been born again, yet surprisingly they remain mastered by some particular habit or temptation or curse from which they can't break free. These people need the supernatural help of the Holy Spirit, help which he provides only when he comes to live within us. According to the Bible, and in particular the Church of England's traditional *Book of Common Prayer*, the Holy Spirit gives Christians victory over the world, the flesh and the devil.

   (i)   <u>The world</u>

The Spirit gives us victory over the temptations of the world by giving us a greater love for God and by taking away our fear of men.

Do not love the world or the things that are in the world. If any one loves the world, love for the Father is not in him.   1 John 2:15

"And now, Lord, look upon their threats, and grant to thy servants to speak thy word with all boldness, while thou stretchest out thy hand to heal, and signs and wonders are performed through the name of thy holy servant Jesus." And when they had prayed, the place in which they were

gathered together was shaken; and they were all filled with the Holy Spirit and spoke the word of God with boldness. Acts 4:29-31

(ii) The flesh

The human part of our nature, which the Bible calls the flesh, comprises our natural instincts for food, drink, sleep, sex and self-preservation. Even as born-again believers, this part of us remains deeply opposed to the will of God. *'For the desires of the flesh are against the Spirit, and the desires of the Spirit are against the flesh.'* (Galatians 5:17) St Peter wrote, *'Beloved, I beseech you as alien and exiles to abstain from the passions of the flesh that wage war against your soul.'* (1 Peter 2:11) And Jesus himself prayed, *"...the spirit is willing, but the flesh is weak."* (Matthew 26:39,41)

Our God-given instinct for self-preservation means that we shrink from any kind of sacrifice or suffering: we put our own welfare first. However, the Lord cannot use us fully while that part of our nature remains in charge. Christ cannot live in us until we have died. This is what Jesus was speaking about when he said, *"If any man would come after me, let him deny himself and take up his cross and follow me. For whoever would save his life will lose it; and whoever loses his life for my sake and the gospel's will save it."* (Mark 8:34,35) But how can we follow in the Master's steps and lay down our lives for his sake? Only the Holy Spirit can enable us to do this. *'For if you live according to the flesh you will die, but if by the Spirit you put to death the deeds of the body you will live.'* (Romans 8:13)

With the help of the indwelling Holy Spirit, we can uproot and destroy the thistles and thorns which our nature keeps producing, and make room in our hearts to grow the fruit which the Holy Spirit produces. *'But the fruit of the Spirit is love, joy, peace, patience, kindness, goodness, faithfulness, gentleness, self-control...'* (Galatians 5:22,23) One could add to this list: faith, hope, humility, obedience, and the willingness to be taught.

Years ago, I knew a Methodist minister who was addicted to smoking a pipe. On the day he was filled with the Holy Spirit he lost all desire to smoke. A similar thing happened to another minister I knew who was addicted to cigarette smoking. A friend of mine, whose marriage broke up because of his alcoholism, never touched a drop of alcohol after the power of the Holy Spirit released him from its hold, and not long afterwards his marriage was restored. Another friend was not only an atheist, but he had a bad temper which would burst out in swear words whenever he became angry. After several months of seeking God, he had a powerful experience of the Holy Spirit in church one Sunday. This not only convinced him of God's reality, but his own personality changed so much that even when he hit his head by walking into a glass door, not even the mildest expletive left his lips.

Obesity and diabetes are two serious health problems in the UK and similar countries. They are generally, but not always, due to eating too much of the wrong kinds of food and drink. The Bible has many warnings about gluttony and drunkenness, which means that they are spiritual problems caused by temptations of the flesh.

One reason people eat too much is that they eat too *little* in the way of protein and fat. Protein and fat satisfy hunger longer than starchy carbohydrates do, but starchy carbohydrates are the mainstay of most people's diets. I've explained the problem in my book *Twenty-First Century Nutrition and Family Health*. After my wife had put into practice the lessons I learned when writing that book, she was allowed to come off thirteen years of medication for Type 2 diabetes: her blood glucose level had returned to an acceptable level.

One way to stop snacking is to stop buying snacks! A more effective way to break an addiction to snacking and overeating is to fast from all food for one entire day per week. Fasting strengthens our spirits by giving them practice at ruling the desires of the flesh. And where our spirits are willing, the Holy Spirit is always at hand to help. After forty days of fasting in the wilderness, *'Jesus returned in the power of the Spirit into Galilee.'* (Luke 4:14)

Even with the help of the Spirit, breaking free from some deep-rooted addiction or lifestyle may involve a battle, perhaps even an extended one. In Luke 9:1 it says that Jesus gave his twelve disciples *'power and authority over all demons and to cure diseases.'* But later in the chapter, these same disciples couldn't cast a terrible evil spirit out of a boy. Jesus appeared to upbraid them for their lack of faith, but in Mark's version of the story he explained, at least in some versions of the Greek text, *"This kind cannot be driven out by anything but prayer and fasting."* You might have to pray and fast, but have faith in God. The battle can be won with the help of God's Spirit in you! *'This is the victory that overcomes the world, our faith.'* (1 John 5:4)

O that we would determine that we shall be ruled by the Spirit and not by the flesh! Let us pray, "Break me, O Lord, break me! Break me, O my God!" until the Lord hears our prayers from on high, and our entire life is recreated in the likeness of his Son!

(iii) <u>The devil</u>

Thirdly, the Spirit gives us victory over the devil.

"Behold, I have given you authority to tread upon serpents and scorpions, and over all the power of the enemy; and nothing shall hurt you."... In that same hour (Jesus) rejoiced in the Holy Spirit...   Luke 10:19,21

I am writing to you young men, because you have overcome the evil one.
1 John 2:13

Resist the devil, and he will flee from you.   James 4:7

When the Holy Spirit dwells in us, we *can* overcome the evil one and live without sin.

He may bring to mind some relevant word of Scripture, as he did for Jesus when he was being tempted in the wilderness. The sword of the Spirit is the word of God. (Ephesians 6:17) The Spirit may reveal some stronghold the devil has over us, through a curse or through something that happened in our past. Sexual abuse in childhood, for example, can have devastating consequences in adult life. He may deliver us from anxiety or depression or even suicidal thoughts, by filling us instead with God's love and joy and peace, as he did for my wife. Or else the Spirit may simply stir us up to fight against some particular injustice or evil that is being perpetrated, enabling us and others to bring it to an end.

'He who is in you is greater than he who is in the world.' (1 John 4:4) You may be born again, but if you continue to be defeated by the world, the flesh or the devil, the reason may simply be that the Holy Spirit is still not in you! He is with you, but not yet in you! (John 14:17)

When I visited people in Chile, they would sometimes smilingly welcome me into their home with the words, "Mi casa es suya," "My house is yours." So welcome the Holy Spirit into your own spirit's house, and go even further. Invite him to take up permanent residence in you, to have access to every room, cupboard and corner, and to make whatever changes he wants to make until you are a dwelling place fit for the Spirit of a holy God.

Chapter 6: Assurance and worship

When we receive the Holy Spirit, he brings us a wonderful assurance of God's love and his acceptance of us; he can transform our personal and corporate times of worship; and the resulting spiritual fruit can draw others to Christ.

The Spirit assures us that we are God's children.

Some people who believe in Jesus Christ are still not sure that their sins are forgiven, or that God really loves them, or that they have a place in his kingdom to come. St John tried to allay such doubts in his first letter. *"The blood of Jesus cleanses us from all sin... In this the love of God was made manifest among us, that God sent his only Son into the world, so that we might live through him... I write this to you who believe in the name of the Son of God, that you may know that you have eternal life.'* (1 John 1:7; 4:9; 5:13)

One thing that distinguishes the Christian faith from every human religion is that when we put our trust in Jesus Christ and in his death for our sins, we have his promise here and now of eternal life. Eternal life is an undeserved gift from God. (Romans 6:23) We do not have to earn it; we do not have to deserve it; we do not have to spend the whole of our life trying to meet a satisfactory standard of behaviour, hoping to achieve a final pass mark on the Day of Judgement. Jesus said, *'Truly, truly, I say to you, he who hears my word and believes him who sent me, has eternal life; he does not come into judgment, but has passed from death to life."* (John 5:24) So believe it! Give thanks to God for his grace and forgiveness and acceptance of you as a believer in Christ your Saviour.

Even so, 'the accuser of the brethren' may try to undermine your faith in God's promises. "Has God really said...?" the devil will whisper. "Surely he can't want someone like *you* in his kingdom?" You can resist the devil as Jesus did by quoting God's promises, but sometimes even that may not be enough to allay our doubts. Difficulties, depression, disaster and death can sometimes lead a Christian to doubt God's love, which may lead to doubting one's salvation. Even the great Martin Luther was constantly beset by such doubts.

There *is* a remedy. It is in the Holy Spirit, the Comforter. *'By this we know that we abide in him and he in us, because he has given us of his own Spirit,'* John wrote. (1 John 4:13) Paul wrote that receiving the Spirit is the seal or guarantee of our inheritance. (Ephesians 1:13) Once God fills us with his Spirit something happens inside us that assures us of God's love for us, that he has truly accepted us as his son or daughter, and that he has assuredly promised us an everlasting inheritance together with his Son.

> *...you have received the spirit of sonship. When we cry, "Abba! Father!" it is the Spirit himself bearing witness with our spirit that we are children of God, and if children, then heirs, heirs of God and fellow heirs with Christ...*
> Romans 8:15-17

Although in the early days I considered myself a Christian, I sometimes used to doubt even God's existence. But since the day his Spirit came into my life, I have never doubted God's existence or his love, nor have I doubted his promise to save me from death and welcome me into everlasting life. When I spontaneously say, "I love you, Father," I know the Spirit is assuring me that I am a child of God. And if I am God's child, I know he will never give me up, nor give up on me.

The Spirit helps us to worship God in private.

When we are filled with the Spirit, love, joy and peace overflow into worship.

And because you are sons, God has sent the Spirit of his Son into our hearts, crying, "Abba! Father!"   Galatians 4:6

...God's love has been poured into our hearts through the Holy Spirit which has been given to us.   Romans 5:5

...you received the word in much affliction, with joy inspired by the Holy Spirit.   1 Thessalonians 1:6

But the fruit of the Spirit is love, joy, peace...   Galatians 5:22

When the Lord baptized me in the Holy Spirit, I could hardly stop telling him, "I love you." (I still do it.) I watched a Baptist deacon being prayed for to receive the Holy Spirit. He was so filled with joy that he couldn't stop laughing! A member of one of my congregations was terrified about a forthcoming hospital operation. I lent her Dennis Bennett's book *Nine o'clock in the morning*. She read it in bed one night and suddenly found herself praising God in tongues. The Spirit filled her with peace and took away all her fear. In hospital in the evening before her operation, she refused the proffered sleeping tablets, saying that she didn't need them!

The ability to pray in tongues is a wonderful aid to genuine worship. Once we have prayed in tongues, we can do so whenever we want to. By this means we can praise God and express our new love for him in a beautiful language, *'a fragrant offering, a sacrifice acceptable and pleasing to God.'* (Philippians 4:18)

I'll say a lot more about tongues later, but exercising this gift in private worship brings us wonderfully near to the Lord, gives us rest and refreshment especially when we are weary or despondent, and strengthens our faith in God, so that we can then pray in our own language with increased confidence, understanding and authority. *'Nay, but by men of strange lips and with an alien tongue the Lord will speak to this people, to whom he has said, "This is rest; give rest to the weary; and this is repose."* (Isaiah 28:11,12) Paul quotes these verses in 1 Corinthians 14:21,22, applying them to speaking in tongues.

'*He who speaks in a tongue edifies himself.*' (1 Corinthians 14:4) The Greek word translated 'edify' means 'to build or repair a house.' We build up our faith and hope and love when we worship God with words the Spirit gives us.

The Spirit helps us to worship God corporately.

The corporate worship of Spirit-filled people can be like a foretaste of heaven! While it includes most of the elements common to every church's worship, it has many additional ones which only the Holy Spirit can provide.

(i) <u>Spirit-filled music</u>

Yesterday's worship at the small village church which I now attend in my retirement was simply beautiful. Because of the limitations imposed by the Covid pandemic, a single lady sang the words of the songs, accompanying herself on a keyboard behind the protection of a transparent screen. This was far from ideal, but she sang and played in such a spirit of worship, surrender and closeness to the Lord that tears came to my eyes. At one point the leader of the service began to sing to the Lord with words and melody which he and the Holy Spirit made up, while the music lady followed his lead on the keyboard.

Paul wrote, '*Where the Spirit of the Lord is, there is freedom.*' (2 Corinthians 3:17) The Psalms are full of admonitions to praise the Lord with all kinds of musical instruments, and even with dancing.

> *Praise him for his mighty deeds; praise him according to his excellent greatness! Praise him with trumpet sound; praise him with lute and harp! Praise him with timbrel and dance; praise him with strings and pipe!*

Praise him with sounding cymbals; praise him with loud clashing cymbals! Let everything that breathes praise the Lord!   Psalm 150:2-6

What enthusiasm and joy and freedom that psalm exudes!

Notice that words of praise should have substance: 'praise him for his mighty deeds; praise him according to his excellent greatness.' Exclaiming "Praise the Lord!" can be good, but it is not in itself praise: it is simply an encouragement to others to praise God, either for what he has done or for who he is.

Church members who can play musical instruments should be encouraged to do so in worship, even if they are not expert musicians. We are a family, not a concert audience. Family members don't demand perfection: they encourage each other to do better. Striving for musical perfection can quench the Spirit.

Good singers should also be involved in leading worship. Psalm 68:25 describes a procession heading for the temple of God, with 'the singers in front, the minstrels last, between them maidens playing timbrels.' In a famous victory over the Moabites and Ammonites, the singers of Judah marched in front of the army proclaiming the Lord's steadfast love. *'And when they began to sing and praise, the Lord set an ambush against the men of Ammon, Moab, and Mount Seir, who had come against Judah, and they were routed.'* (2 Chronicles 20:22) The devil can't stand genuine praise. *'God is enthroned on the praises of Israel.'* (Psalm 22:3) Praise somehow frees God to act, as the next two verses in that Psalm declared.

Above all, singers and musicians should be focussed on the Lord rather than on the congregation, and be open to the Spirit's leading as well as to each other.

(ii) <u>Singing in the Spirit</u>

This occurs when people sing together, allowing the Holy Spirit to supply both words and music! Even tone-deaf persons can sometimes sing in harmony, and together it sounds like a choir of angels! '*...be filled with the Spirit, addressing one another in psalms and hymns and spiritual songs, singing and making melody to the Lord with all your heart...*' (Ephesians 5:18,19) Revelation 5:9-14 paints a wonderful picture of such joyful worship in heaven.

(iii) <u>Prophecy</u>

When we pray, we speak to God: when someone prophesies, God speaks to us. It is awe-inspiring and humbling to hear the voice of God, a voice of majesty, tenderness, and intimate understanding of our individual personalities and needs.

Comfort, comfort my people, says your God. Speak tenderly to Jerusalem, and cry to her that her warfare is ended, that her iniquity is pardoned, that she has received from the Lord's hand double for all her sins.

Isaiah 40:1,2

...he who prophesies speaks to men for their upbuilding and encouragement and consolation... He who prophesies edifies the church... if all prophesy, and an unbeliever or outsider enters, he is convicted by all, the secrets of his heart are disclosed; and so, falling on his face, he will worship God and declare that God is really among you.

1 Corinthians 14:3,4,24,25

Through Spirit-inspired prophecy God gives direction to his church as a whole, and sometimes to individual members of it. I was struggling to write my first published Christian book, *Z: The Final Generation,* but one Sunday morning a man who didn't know me well or what I was doing stood up in church and said, "Arnold, sometimes you get discouraged. God wants to encourage you to persist. He says it's good stuff you are doing." Afterwards he said those were the first words that came to him when he woke up that day!

(iv) Visions

And in the last days it shall be, God declares, that I will pour out my Spirit upon all flesh, and your sons and your daughters shall prophesy, and your young men shall see visions, and your old men shall dream dreams...
                                        Acts 2:17, quoting Joel 2:28

Besides prophecies, the Holy Spirit speaks through visions. Originally prophets were called seers, because the Lord made them see pictures of the future. (e.g., Jeremiah 1:13-16)

Near Belfast in Northern Ireland is a small town called Holywood. It suffered at least two terrorist bombs during the so-called troubles. In a Sunday morning service I attended there, three people in turn had a vision, and two more its interpretation. One saw a crown in the sky; another saw flames sweeping across the earth underneath the crown; and a third saw plants, shrubs and flowers springing up in the flames where rain was falling. A fourth person said the crown meant that Jesus was Lord, that the flames stood for violence and death, and that the rain was a promise that God would bring the troubles to an end. A fifth person said he believed the rain was tears. Jesus was weeping over the suffering, and when his people cared enough to weep for their countrymen, and when they would unite beneath the lordship of Christ to pray with tears, then life would no longer be destroyed, and the flames of violence would be quenched.

In this simple and beautiful way, the Holy Spirit enabled five people to make a precious contribution to the worship of the Lord, and eventually the troubles did cease.

As with prophecy, the Lord can use visions to speak to individuals, as well as to the church as a whole. In my last year of training as a Methodist minister, I felt called to work overseas. My wife and I decided it would be best for me to take an initial appointment in England and apply for overseas service once we had gained a little experience. So in 1970, towards the end of my first appointment in Norfolk, we arranged to be interviewed in London by the then Methodist Missionary Society.

Before we went, I asked a minister friend to pray with us. We wanted to ask the Lord if there was any particular country he wanted us to go to. Soon after I started to pray, Ann received a series of incredibly clear visions. She described them as she saw them - snow-covered mountains and volcanoes, an old steam train, and a number of close-up scenes of rural life with people who looked like native Americans. She saw a map of South America, then of Chile, and then what was probably a *preview* of the celebrations by Salvador Allende's supporters following his election as Chile's first Marxist president. (Similar scenes were shown on television a few months later.)

The Lord immediately confirmed that these visions were from him by telling our minister friend to read Isaiah chapter 49.

"You read it and we'll listen," I said.

It wasn't that David recalled what was in Isaiah 49. In any case, he didn't think I should be a missionary at all before we began to pray that day! Yet the first six verses in particular were amazingly appropriate. They concluded, *"I will give you as a light to the nations, that my salvation may reach to the end of the earth."*

Two days later I borrowed a book about Chile from the public library. In the very first paragraph it said, 'The name "Chile" is believed to have been derived from a Mapuche word meaning "place where the land ends" or *"the end of the earth."*

(v) Words of knowledge

Included in Paul's list of gifts that the Holy Spirit gives, the Greek text of 1 Corinthians 12:8 has 'a word of knowledge.' This is a supernatural revelation by the Spirit of some fact God wants us to know and make use of. Its purpose can be:

- to lead someone to Christ
- to restore a believer back to fellowship with God
- to reveal the root cause of a spiritual, mental or physical condition
- to reveal a sickness that God is ready to heal through a prayer of faith
- to resolve a difficult problem
- to provide encouragement.

One Saturday evening at an evangelistic meeting in Santiago, the Bible teacher Mike Darwood asked me to help him by means of a mime. Basing his message on words from Psalm 107, '*He sent forth his word and healed them, and delivered them from destruction,*' he wanted me to act the part of a prisoner condemned to death who was given a last-minute written reprieve. A written note was handed to him, saying that all the charges against him had been dropped. But instead of walking out a free man, he remained shivering with fear in his cell, unable to believe he had been pardoned. Mike wanted to show us that to receive God's blessings of healing or deliverance or eternal salvation, we have to believe what he has promised. Otherwise, we shall remain prisoners, even though the door to our cell has been unlocked.

I asked Mike if he could say that the man's execution was to be in five days' time, so that as he counted off the days to his death on his fingers, he could become more and more fearful. I suggested that as the last day approached, he would sink to his knees, praying more and more fervently for deliverance, even though he would not initially believe it when it came. Of course, when the truth of his pardon finally sank in, his joy would know no bounds.

The story was duly told to a hushed audience. When I sat down, the evangelist Don Double whispered to me, "That was prophetic!"

Don's verdict proved to be true, for the five days which I'd requested turned out to have been a word of knowledge from the Lord. Five days previously two young men named Felipe and Francisco had been caught stealing a rifle from the back of a police car. This was during President Pinochet's military dictatorship, when thousands of his political opponents had 'disappeared', so the two brothers were in serious trouble!

Before their arrest, their mother had wanted them to attend the meeting that Saturday, because neither of her two boys was yet saved. When she heard they had been imprisoned, she prayed for them, and she was allowed to give them a Bible. One brother refused to read it, blaming God for allowing them to get caught! The other, like the repentant thief who was crucified with Jesus, acknowledged his wrongdoing. He prayed for forgiveness and asked God to help him amend his life.

Early the following Saturday, after exactly five days in jail, a warder entered their cell and announced that they had been granted a provisional pardon. They were free to go, just like the prisoner in the mime! On returning home, their mother insisted that they came to the meeting that evening to give thanks to God for their pardon, and to promise him that they would amend their lives.

As you can imagine, Felipe and Francisco watched the mime incredulously, as it almost told the story of their last few days. And when Don invited people to come forward and commit their lives to Christ, they practically jumped out of their seats. One of them (I forget which) was also baptized in the Spirit then and there, and praised God in tongues.

When Jesus was talking to the Samaritan woman by the well of Sychar, their conversation wasn't getting very far until he said to her, *"You have had five husbands, and he whom you now have is not your husband."* That word of knowledge convinced the woman that Jesus was a prophet, and through her witness to the townspeople, many came to believe Jesus was the promised Saviour of the world. (John 4:16-19,42)

Another time in Chile I was in our town centre when the Lord said to me, "Ann needs you." I didn't hear an audible voice, but the words were clear in my head. So instead of carrying on with what I was doing, I returned home to my wife, only to discover that our house had just caught fire. Ann was fast asleep upstairs having a siesta, and the children were playing in their bedrooms, oblivious of the flames from the kitchen that had just reached the staircase. That word of knowledge saved the lives of my family.

How important it is always to keep alert for that still, small voice of the Lord!

Jesus promised the Samaritan woman, *'The hour is coming, and now is, when the true worshippers will worship the Father in spirit and truth..."* (John 4:23) In most Christian worship there is plenty of truth but not much evidence of the Spirit. What I mean is that if the Holy Spirit went on holiday, most worship could continue in exactly the same way without him! The Holy Spirit wants to speak to us about Jesus; he wants to glorify Jesus; he wants to make us like Jesus is; and he has gifts to give us, so that we can minister to each other for the common good. (John 16:14; Galatians 5:5; 1 Corinthians 12:7-10)

For these things to happen, the Spirit must have freedom to direct at least part of the proceedings. Paul tells us it's possible to quench the Spirit (1 Thessalonians 5:19), and that's what happens when every detail of a church service is planned, or it is conducted throughout with set rituals so that the Spirit has no way in to do something different. In many churches it's as though the entire service has been treated with a spiritual flame retardant.

Worship leaders must give the Holy Spirit the freedom he needs to bring everyone into the presence of Jesus. *'Now the Lord is the Spirit, and where the Spirit of the Lord is, there is freedom.'* (2 Corinthians 3:17) This doesn't mean everyone can do as they like, or that everybody may talk at once, but that we give the Lord freedom to do what he wants. Even when people receive a word of prophecy from the Lord, they must still await their turn. *'For you can all prophesy one by one, so that all may learn and all be encouraged; and the spirits of the prophets are subject to prophets. For God is not a God of confusion, but of peace.'* (1 Corinthians 14.31-33)

Leading worship under the direction of the Holy Spirit requires wisdom, faith, sensitivity and boldness on the part of a worship leader. In most churches, worship leaders need to encourage people constantly to participate in the manifestation of spiritual gifts, both leading by example and by making space for everyone else to contribute. They have to *tell* people it's OK to sing in the spirit, or to share a picture or thought they believe God has given them, or to bring a message in tongues if they don't have the faith to prophesy directly. Sometimes it may be right for everyone simply to wait on the Lord in silence for a while. (Psalm 62:1,5)

Because true worship is in both spirit and truth, corporate worship should normally include teaching from the Scriptures, with practical applications of the teaching to people's lives. (James 1:22-25) Such teaching might be from a prepared address, or it might be delivered spontaneously with the help of the Holy Spirit. Whichever way it is done, it would often be good after delivering it to invite comments and questions from the rest of the congregation. We can encourage each other by sharing something from the message with partcular meaning for us, or by adding something from our own experience which confirms the teaching. (Hebrews 10:25) This could be a means of identifying future pastors or teachers.

When Jesus taught, he also healed the sick. On several occasions he healed or delivered someone during a synagogue service. (Matthew 4:23; Mark 3:1-6; Mark 1:21-28) Hebrews tells us he is the same yesterday, today and forever. So worship leaders and preachers should always be open to the possibility that the Lord might want to heal someone or deliver someone from some bondage during a meeting.

One Sunday morning I was taking a service of Holy Communion. As the congregation came up one by one to receive the bread and wine, I felt a strong urge to lay hands on one particular lady and pray for her healing. I didn't know anything was wrong with her, but I did it anyway.

After the service she said, "I'm so glad you prayed for me. Yesterday I threw away all my anti-depression medication and resolved to trust God to make me better."

Think what would happen if Jesus were to attend our church service in the flesh one Sunday. I imagine we would first be awestruck; then we would want hear what he had to say; and then, I am sure, we would ask him to heal us if we were suffering from an incurable disease or if we had some serious physical or mental disability. We would, wouldn't we? But didn't Jesus promise that when we gather together, he *will* be in our midst? (Matthew 18:20) So why don't we act as if we believe it!

Jesus said, *"Learn from me"* (Matthew 11:29), and the crowds flocked to hear Jesus because of the miracles he did. People always turn up when Jesus is healing people. T. L. Osborn, for example, who died in 2013 after a long life, believed in the power of God to heal the sick. Crowds of up to 300,000 came to his crusades, which he held in over 80 different nations. In one crusade in Jamaica 125 deaf-mutes and 90 blind people were healed, along with thousands of conversions to Christ. And in the 1950s up to 400 new churches a year were being planted through his ministry. There are several YouTube videos of Osborn's preaching when he was old. Jesus came to make us whole in body, mind and spirit, and that should be in the mind of all Christian preachers.

Of course, praying for healing and deliverance has to spring from faith, which itself is a gift of the Spirit. Sometimes there are blockages which must first be cleared away, and discovering them may need the gift of discernment. (James 5:14-16; Mark 2:3-12) But we are worshipping a living Lord, who promised that his Spirit would teach us all things. (John 14:26) Jesus said, *"A disciple is not above his teacher, but every one when he is fully taught will be like his teacher."* (Luke 6:40)

Chapter 7: The fruit of the Spirit

The fruit of the Spirit – Christian character

The thought of becoming like Jesus brings us to the fruit of the Spirit. In the New Testament, the fruit of the Spirit has two very different meanings. The first of these is a Christ-like character.

As I've already said, Paul described the fruit of the Spirit as love, joy, peace, patience, kindness, goodness, faithfulness, gentleness and self-control.

Jesus Christ was filled with love, not only for those who were easy to love but for the unlovable too, and even for those who opposed him. He told his disciples, *"Greater love has no man this, that a man lay down his life for his friends."* (John 15:13) '*...and not for ours only but also for the sins of the whole world.*' (1 John 2:2)

Jesus also possessed joy and peace. He continued, *"These things I have spoken to you, that my joy may be in you, and that your joy may be full."* (John 15:11) *"Peace I leave with you; my peace I give to you."* (John 14:27)

And it goes without saying, though of course I am going to say it anyway, that Jesus was also patient, kind, good, faithful, gentle and self-controlled, even if some of these attributes did get a bit stretched when he was driving the money-changers out of the temple!

If you are going through a hard time just now, you might be tempted to excuse yourself from feeling particularly joyful or peaceful. And if it's someone else who is giving you a hard time, you are probably not feeling very loving towards them either. I can only point out that when Jesus offered his love and joy and peace to his friends, he knew full well he would be arrested that very night and would be taken off to be crucified. Only the Holy Spirit can work such a miracle in someone. Ask him to do the same for you!

Praise God that the new birth itself often produces such lovely fruit in a person's life. But just as earthly fruit takes time to ripen in the warmth of the sun, so the same qualities that were evident in Jesus's life can increase in us over time, so long as we remain filled with the Holy Spirit who is their source.

Spiritual fruit is vital for making disciples. A tree grows fruit to attract people or other creatures to eat it and thereby to propagate its seeds so that more trees can grow. When our lives radiate the fruit of the Spirit, it draws people to us. They become receptive to the gospel when we share it with them, because they want to be like us. An obvious love for them, a joyful personality, and a peaceful demeanour are bound to make our message more attractive and desirable than one delivered from a judgemental attitude, with a miserable face and an impatient manner.

Earlier this year, my daughter was assisting a street evangelist by handing out gospel tracts. One lady said to her, "I don't really want one, but I will take it because you have such a lovely smile!" This is a simple but perfect illustration of what Paul wrote in Romans 14:17: *'For the kingdom of God is not food and drink but righteousness and peace and joy in the Holy Spirit; he who thus serves Christ is acceptable to God and approved by men.'* The fruit of the Spirit is to attract sinners to Christ.

So when you are struggling, don't let the devil rob you of love, joy, peace or anything else that's good. Paul reminded the Thessalonian believers, *'...you received the word in much affliction, with joy inspired by the Holy Spirit...'* (1 Thessalonians 1:6) The Holy Spirit is the source of unquenchable joy, peace and hope:

> *We rejoice in our hope of sharing the glory of God. More than that, we rejoice in our sufferings, knowing that suffering produces endurance, and endurance produces character, and character produces hope, and hope does not disappoint us, because God's love has been poured into our hearts through the Holy Spirit who has been given to us... May the God of hope*

fill you with all joy and peace in believing, so that by the power of the Holy Spirit you may abound in hope. Romans 5:2-5; 15:13

The whole point of this mortal life is to prepare for God's promise of everlasting life in all its fullness in the world to come. Keep your eyes on the goal!

The fruit of the Spirit – Christian offspring

Now we come to the other kind of spiritual fruit. In the Old Testament God was very concerned that people should be physically fruitful and multiply, especially his chosen people! He told Adam and Eve, Noah and his sons, Abraham, Jacob and even Ishmael to be fruitful and multiply. Exodus 1:7 says that *'the descendants of Israel were fruitful and increased greatly; they multiplied and grew exceedingly strong; so that the land was filled with them.'* In the Old Testament, wherever being fruitful refers to people, it always means having many human offspring.

However, when Jesus spoke about being fruitful, he meant producing many *spiritual* offspring. Speaking of his forthcoming crucifixion, he said, *"The hour has come for the Son of man to be glorified. Truly, truly, I say to you, unless a grain of wheat falls into the earth and dies it remains alone; but if it dies, it bears much fruit."* Isaiah had made the same point: *'When he makes himself an offering for sin, he shall see his offspring… he shall see the fruit of the travail of his soul and be satisfied…'* (Isaiah 53:10,11) The fruit of Christ's travail on the cross is the church!

Think about the parable of the sower. Much of the sower's seed fell on barren ground, but *"other seeds fell on good soil and brought forth grain, some a hundredfold, some sixty, and some thirty."* (Matthew 13:8) We tend to think of this story as an encouragement to evangelists to keep spreading God's word, in the knowledge that some of it at least will bear fruit. But that wasn't really Jesus's point. He was saying that the kingdom of God increases when those who believe his teaching each produce multiple new believers. Hear how he explained the meaning of the parable. *"As for what was sown on good soil, <u>this is he</u> who hears the word and understands it; <u>he</u> indeed bears much fruit, and yields, in one case a hundredfold, in another sixty, and in another thirty."* (Matthew 13:23) Just as single grain of wheat can produce a hundred more, so someone who hears and believes the teaching of Jesus can, with God's help, produce many more believers.

Now we can understand what Jesus meant by fruit when he addressed his disciples at the Last Supper.

"He who abides in me, and I in him, he it is that bears much fruit, for apart from me you can do nothing... By this my Father is glorified, that you bear much fruit, and so prove to be my disciples... You did not choose me, but I chose you and appointed you that you should go and bear fruit and that your fruit should abide..." John 15:5,8,16

The words 'that you should go and bear fruit' are the equivalent of Jesus's command in Matthew's gospel, *"Go therefore, and make disciples of all nations..."* (Matthew 28:19)

What a challenge all this is! It is indisputable that when Jesus tells us to abide in him so that we can bear much fruit he means that every one of us who abides in him should lead many others to believe in him and become his disciples, *'some a hundredfold, some sixty, and some thirty'*!

That is how the early Christians were fruitful and multiplied. Early in Paul's first missionary journey, he preached the gospel to some Gentiles (non-Jews) in a town named Antioch of Pisidia. *'And when the Gentiles heard this, they were glad and glorified the word of God; and as many as were ordained to eternal life believed. And the word of the Lord spread throughout all the region.'* (Acts 13: 48,49) How did it spread? Not through Paul and Barnabas. They were driven out of the city at the instigation of the unbelieving Jewish leaders and went off to Iconium. It can only have been through the excited testimony of the new believers in Christ, who *'were filled with joy and with the Holy Spirit.'* (Acts 13:52)

Being 'filled with joy and with the Holy Spirit' is essential, I believe, to effectively sharing the gospel and producing spiritual offspring. It is essential, both to motivate us to do it, and to convince those we talk to that we are offering them some truly good news. King David prayed, 'Take not thy Holy Spirit from me. Restore to me the joy of thy salvation, and uphold me with a willing spirit. Then I will teach transgressors thy ways, and sinners will return to thee.' (Psalm 51:11-13) That's a prayer which most of us who believe in Jesus need to pray, and we need to keep praying it until the Lord answers.

Jesus's address at the last supper gives us another clue as to how we can be fruitful in making disciples. He said, *'If you abide in me, and my words abide in you, ask whatever you will, and it shall be done for you. By this my Father is glorified, that you bear much fruit, and so prove to be my disciples."* (John 15:7,8) 'Ask whatever you will... that you bear much fruit.' There is a link between the two...

When I was a Methodist minister, I was told that a couple wanted their baby to be baptized, so I went to visit them. The young mother was in, but she didn't seem particularly pleased to see me.

"I understand you'd like me to baptize your baby," I began.

"It's my mother-in-law who wants it done," she replied, stubbing out a cigarette.

"I see. What's your baby's name?"

She told me. And then she said, "She's sick. She hasn't eaten anything for a day and just now she sicked up her milk. I think I'll have to take her to the doctor's."

"I'm really sorry about that. May I pray for her?"

She shrugged her shoulders. "If you want."

So I did.

At that time, I still conducted services of infant baptism, so I arranged a Sunday for the service to take place and I left the house. There didn't seem to be much point in taking the conversation any further at that moment.

A few days later, I met the same woman in the street.

"When you came to my house, I didn't believe in God," she began. "My cousin was killed in the Aberfan disaster. When that slag heap fell on top of the school and buried nearly all the children, I couldn't believe in God any more. But after you prayed, I did what you said in your prayer, and it all happened like you prayed."

"What did I pray?" I asked, apprehensively. I try to let the Spirit lead me when I pray, so I don't always remember what I've said.

"You prayed that next time I gave her some milk she'd be able to keep it down, and then tomorrow she'd be able to sit up and have something to eat. So I had another go with some milk, and it was OK. So then I thought I'd try with a little bit of food, and that was OK too. She's been all right since. So I do believe in God again, because he answered your prayer!"

"If you abide in me, and my words abide in you, ask whatever you will, and it shall be done for you. By this my Father is glorified..." Jesus worked many miracles through the power of the Spirit, so when we are filled with the Spirit, we should be able to do the same. When we have the courage to do so, it opens the door for people to believe in God and receive the gospel. And so, with the Spirit's help, we become fruitful.

Chapter 8: Empowered to do God's will

Supernatural gifts

The Holy Spirit distributes supernatural gifts such as healings, words of knowledge, prophecy and messages in tongues, in order to reveal the lordship of Jesus Christ over all things, to demonstrate God's saving power and love, and to convince unbelievers of the truth. *"He (the Spirit of truth) will glorify me, for he will take what is mine and declare it to you."* (John 16:14) *'All these [gifts] are inspired by one and the same Spirit, who apportions to each one individually as he wills.'* (1 Corinthians 12:11)

Now here's a question: if the Holy Spirit decides which gifts we are to have, why does Paul encourage us to *'earnestly desire the spiritual gifts, especially that you may prophesy'*? (1 Corinthians 14:1) Why does he write, *'He who speaks in a tongue should pray for the power to interpret'*? (1 Corinthians 14.13) What is the point of desiring a particular gift or praying for it if the Spirit decides who gets what?

While the Spirit distributes such gifts, the gifts themselves come from the Father. (James 1:17) And whether we receive something special from the Father depends as always on our relationship with him and what we want it for.

If a child wants something very much and pleads for his father to give it to him, if the father sees it is good for the child to have it he will usually give it. On the other hand, if he knows that the child's desire is only a passing desire and that after a while he would lose interest and cast the gift aside, then the father will probably not give it. That's why Paul writes *'earnestly* desire the spiritual gifts...'

Secondly, neither the Father nor the Holy Spirit will equip us with some gift we ask for, however insistently, if our motive for using is self-promotion. The spiritual gifts are to glorify Jesus, not ourselves. As

James wrote, 'You ask and do not receive, because you ask wrongly, to spend it on your passions.' (James 4:3)

If you feel strongly drawn to exercise some particular spiritual gift, and if you really want to make use of it in the service of the Lord, then it may be that the Spirit himself has planted that desire within you. The Bible gives you permission to ask for it and to keep on asking, until either you receive it or God clearly says "No." Jesus promised God will give us good gifts if we ask for them, so ask in faith. It's what he wants you to do!

This teaching is supported by two different accounts of what Jesus taught concerning prayer. In Matthew 7:11 Jesus says, *"If you then, who are evil, know how to give good gifts to your children, how much more will your Father who is in heaven give good things to those who ask him!"* However, Luke reports what presumably was the same teaching, as follows: *"If you then, who are evil, know how to give good gifts to your children, how much more will the heavenly Father give the Holy Spirit to those who ask him!"* (Luke 11:13)

It seems that while Jesus was encouraging us to pray both for good gifts in general and for the Holy Spirit in particular, he also had in mind those spiritual gifts the Holy Spirit gives for building up the body of Christ in all the different ways it needs. Therefore, we can and should ask for a spiritual gift that we would love to exercise, in the expectation that our heavenly Father will grant our request if we earnestly desire it, and if it is good for us to have it for the benefit of the church or outsiders.

We all have natural gifts of one kind or another, perhaps hospitality or guitar playing or speaking foreign languages or playing football. But however good we are at something, we always improve with practice. It's the same with spiritual gifts. A gift may be supernatural, but with practice we can improve the way we use it.

Finally, although Paul writes about these gifts in the context of church worship, the gifts of the Spirit are just as much for use in the world to lead people to faith in Christ, perhaps even more so.

Nepal is a mountainous country sandwiched between China and India. Some 80% of its 30 million population are Hindus, and back in 1960 there were only 30 known Christians there. But in a 2018 *Report on International Religious Freedom* published by the United States Department of State, it was estimated that the number of Nepalese Christians had increased to around 3 million: 10% of the population! When the Evangelical Alliance's ambassador Brian Stiller asked local leaders why so many people had converted to Christ, he was told there were two vital factors: physical healing and deliverance from the control of evil spirits through the prayers of Spirit-filled Christians.

Similarly, Canon Douglas Milmine of the former South American Missionary Society reported that the astonishing growth of the Pentecostal churches in Chile during the early twentieth century was due largely to church members praying for sick friends and neighbours to be healed. We could do the same!

Paul himself wrote, *'I will not venture to speak of anything except what Christ has wrought through me to win obedience from the Gentiles, by word and deed, by the power of signs and wonders, by the power of the Holy Spirit...'* (Romans 15:18,19) And the author of Hebrews wrote that the gospel message *'was declared at first by the Lord, and it was attested to us by those who heard him, while God also bore witness by signs and wonders and various miracles and by gifts of the Holy Spirit distributed according to his own will.'* (Hebrews 2: 3,4)

If you long to lead people to Christ, don't pray only for boldness and love and wisdom, but pray also for supernatural gifts such as words of knowledge and prophecy, gifts of special faith, the discernment of spirits, and perhaps above all, of healing.

The Spirit enables us to testify to Christ.

'That which we have seen and heard we proclaim also to you.' (1 John 1:3) It's easy to talk about such a wonderful person as Jesus Christ when you

have met him personally! When we worship the Lord Jesus in the Spirit, he becomes so real to us that it's easy to speak about him to other people. That's what the Samaritan woman did, and as a result the people in her village wanted to meet Jesus too!

> *So the woman left her water jar, and went away into the city, and said to the people, "Come, see a man who told me all that I ever did. Can this be the Christ?" They went out of the city and were coming to him.*
>
> John 4:28-30

Shyness, timidity and fear are hindrances to effective witnessing. We want people to like us; we don't want to upset them or spoil our relationship with them; and we don't want people to think we are weird. We may fear becoming tongue-tied or fear being asked questions we can't answer. I think Paul's young disciple Timothy experienced such feelings. For Timothy the solution was to be refilled with the Holy Spirit.

> *Hence I remind you to rekindle the gift of God that is within you through the laying on of my hands; for God did not give us a spirit of timidity but a spirit of power and love and self-control. Do not be ashamed then of testifying to our Lord...*
>
> 2 Timothy 1:6-8

The name 'Timothy' meant 'God fearer.' Paul wanted Timothy to fear God rather than men.

Being filled with the Spirit is not a once-only event. In Acts 4:31 the first Christians were filled again with the Holy Spirit, and in Ephesians 5:18 Paul urges the Ephesians Christians to 'be filled with the Spirit.' (Literally, 'go on being filled with the Spirit.') That's why he told Timothy to rekindle the flame of the Spirit which he had once received.

Usually, the Spirit is initially given through a belief in God's promises and prayer. Jesus said that we may ask the Father to give his Spirit to us, so we can pray for ourself. In the New Testament, however, people were more often filled with the Spirit when they were praying together or when someone else prayed for them. (Galatians 3:2; Luke 11:13; Acts 4:31; 19:6) We receive the Spirit through believing prayer, and we rekindle the gift in the same way. So let's do it! *"Ask (and keep on asking) and it will be given you!"* (Luke 11:9)

Paul tells Timothy that when we are filled with the Holy Spirit, three things happen:

(i) <u>We are filled with power and boldness.</u>

When I came to you, brethren... I was with you in much fear and trembling; and my speech and my message were not in plausible words of wisdom, but in demonstration of the Spirit and power...

1 Corinthians 2:1-4

Now when they saw the boldness of Peter and John, and perceived that they were uneducated, common men, they wondered; and they recognized that they had been with Jesus. Acts 4:13

Pray at all times in the Spirit, with all prayer and supplication... for all the saints, and also for me, that utterance may be given me in opening my mouth boldly to proclaim the mystery of the gospel...

Ephesians 6:18-20

(ii) <u>We are filled with love.</u>

God's love has been poured into our hearts through the Holy Spirit which has been given to us. Romans 5:5

When the Spirit gives us the Father's own heart for lost sinners, we stop thinking about ourselves, and we think about them instead. He helps us to realize how much Jesus suffered to save *us* from our sins, and that he also died for others who will not be saved unless someone tells them.

For the love of Christ controls us, because we are convinced that one has died for all; therefore all have died. And he died for all, that those who live might live no longer for themselves but for him who for their sake died and was raised.　　　　　　　　　　　　　　　　　　　2 Corinthians 5:14,15

When we have even a little of God's love for lost sinners, we long for them to know Jesus and be saved from final death.

(iii) <u>We become self-disciplined.</u>

The Greek word translated in 2 Timothy chapter 1 as self-control or a sound mind can also mean self-discipline. In the next chapter Paul expanded on this by reminding Timothy that soldiers, athletes and farmers all need self-discipline: they have to train and work hard to produce results. So what was in Paul's mind at this point? Having urged Timothy to rekindle the flame of God's Spirit within him, he wrote, '*Do not be ashamed then of testifying to our Lord...*'

That word 'then' shows that in Paul's mind the main purpose of being refilled with the Spirit was to enable Timothy to testify to Jesus: to tell people about Jesus's life and death and resurrection, and about his offer to everyone of salvation from sin, judgement and death through faith in him. Jesus himself said that the Spirit would enable his apostles to become effective witnesses. (Acts 1:8)

The reason the Holy Spirit enables us to testify to Jesus is not only that he fills us with boldness and love but also that he supplies us with the self-discipline we need in order to work at sharing our testimony effectively. The harder we work at sharing our testimony to Christ, the more effective we'll be able to do it. Elsewhere, Paul writes about the 'preparation' of the gospel of peace (Ephesians 6:15), while Peter tells us always to be prepared to explain why we hope to live forever. (1 Peter 3:15) We need self-discipline to prepare ourselves to share our testimony, and that self-discipline is a third fruit of the Spirit.

If we really want to share the gospel effectively, most of us do have to put some effort into thinking out how to explain it, how to tell our story of coming to faith in Jesus and what difference he has made, learning some relevant scriptures, and thinking how best we can reach people through our own particular personality, abilities and opportunities.

At the start of this year (as I write), a friend of mine wanted to be a street evangelist. He began reading the New Testament right through once a week, and he did this so many times that he lost count! Here's what he wrote to me the other day:

Every day I speak in tongues through the day. Yesterday some very stressful situations came along, and I spoke more than ever because of the massive attacks. Speaking in tongues is like nitrous oxide in an engine for me. My boldness went through the roof. Everywhere I went I preached, to the driver filling his car up next to me, at the cashier's desk, at a reception and then at another cashier's desk, etc.

I went to a key kiosk and challenged an atheist with what God has given every one of us to bring us to him – the fear of death. He denied he was scared of death, but he recanted after I embellished what death really means...

I preached to him God's holy laws in our hearts and heads (Hebrews 10: 16); a God-given conscience that separates us from the beasts of the field (Romans 2:15); our inability to pay the wages of sin and survive its penalty of eternal death (Romans 6:23); and the knowledge of God through creation that witnesses to everyone, so that we shall be without excuse when the appointed day of judgement comes to all of us (Romans 1:20 and Hebrews 9: 27).

I would not back down: his soul was too precious to God. I polemically stood my ground. He realized at last that he needed a Saviour, and he received the gospel.

The Spirit enables us to know God's will.

Jesus promised his apostles, *"When the Spirit of truth comes, he will guide you into all the truth."* (John 16:13)

If men who had been learning from Jesus himself for two or three years still needed the Holy Spirit to teach them what to do and say, how much more must we! Jesus told them that the Spirit would lead them into *all* the truth. What a promise! And he promises to do the same for you and me! If you have been anointed with the Spirit of truth, you don't need a degree in theology to know all the truth about God you need to know! 'The anointing which you received from him abides in you, and you have no need that anyone should teach you; as his anointing teaches you about everything...' (1 John 2:27)

The anointing of the Holy Spirit:

- enables us to understand God's Word (1 Corinthians 2:9-12)
- enables God to give direct, specific guidance to us when it is necessary (Acts 10:19,20)
- reveals the secrets of men's hearts (Acts 5:1-4; 1 Corinthians 14:24,25)
- reveals the future to us so that we can plan accordingly (Acts 11:27-30)
- enables God to keep us in his will (Acts 16:6-10)
- shows us what to believe and say and do, when naturally we would not know (1 Corinthians 12:8,9a).

Examples of this in the life of Jesus are seen in Matthew 22:15-46. Jesus knew everything he needed to know to do his Father's will perfectly, but only because he was anointed with the Holy Spirit. (Isaiah 11:2-5) If the Son of God needed the Spirit's anointing to know the Father's will, how can we expect to know God's will without the same anointing?

The Spirit enables us to do God's will.

And Jesus went about all the cities and villages, teaching in their synagogues and preaching the gospel of the kingdom, and healing every disease and every infirmity. Matthew 9:35

"I always do what is pleasing to [my Father]." John 8:29

These two verses show us that teaching people how to enter God's kingdom, and healing the sick in body, mind and heart, are both activities which please God. What is the will of God? He 'wants all men to be saved and to come to the knowledge of the truth.' (1 Timothy 2:3) 'God so loved the world that he gave his only Son, that whoever believes in him should not perish but have eternal life.' (John 3:16)

Because Jesus was full of his Father's love, he too longed to see every single person saved from sin and from all its terrible consequences. He wanted to gather the entire world into his Father's kingdom. *"I lay down my life for the sheep. And I have other sheep, that are not of this fold. I must bring them also, and they will heed my voice. So there shall be one flock, one shepherd."* (John 10:15,16) *"For the Son of man came to seek and to save the lost."* (Luke 19:10)

Jesus Christ is currently in heaven, but his ministry has not changed, neither has his Father's will changed. The difference is that now Jesus seeks the lost, he preaches and teaches and heals and delivers people, *through us*. He wants us, his disciples, to continue his work, to continue to do the same sorts of things as he did. *"Truly, truly, I say to you, he who believes in me will also do the works that I do."* (John 14:12)

Even Jesus had to be anointed by the Holy Spirit in order to heal the sick and work other miracles. *"...God anointed Jesus of Nazareth with the Holy Spirit and with power... he went about doing good and healing all that were oppressed by the devil, for God was with him."* (Acts 10:38) By returning to the Father after his resurrection, Jesus was able to send the Holy Spirit to us. *"...It is to your advantage that I go away, for if I do not go away, the Counsellor will not come to you; but if I go, I will send him to you."* (John 16:7) Jesus said that we'd then be able to do even greater works than he did. *"He who believes in me will also do the works that I do; and greater works than these will he do, because I go to the Father."*

Jesus was one solitary person confined to one place, but we can do what he did in our thousands and millions all over the earth. The tragedy is that instead of multiplying Christ's ministry, we more often limit it. Either we don't believe he will fulfil his promises, or else we don't seriously want him to. If the sight of sinners unaware that they are heading for hell or of sick people suffering from incurable diseases doesn't send us to our knees in prayer for the power to help them we are not much better than the Pharisees of Jesus's day, who didn't want him to heal a man whose hand was withered. Jesus, we are told, looked round at them with anger, grieved by the hardness of their hearts. (Mark 3:5) I fear that we too may be breaking his heart when we don't care enough for the lost to want to help them with the power that's available to us in him, for there is no other personal way in which Jesus can reach people today.

The Father wants us to continue the work his Son began. We can do this, but only by praying for and receiving the gift of the Holy Spirit, just as Jesus himself did at the beginning of his ministry. So let's do it! There is no other way. For it is *'not by might, nor by power, but by my Spirit, says the Lord of hosts.'* (Zechariah 4:6)

Chapter 9: Some questions about speaking in tongues

Are 'tongues' real languages?

The Greek word which is usually translated in the New Testament as 'tongues' means simply 'languages.' 'Speaking in tongues' therefore means 'speaking in languages given by the Holy Spirit.' In teaching about this subject, Paul writes, *'There are doubtless many different languages in the world, and none is without meaning.'* (1 Corinthians 14:10) And he writes, *'If I speak in the tongues of men and of angels....'* (1 Corinthians 13:1) So Paul taught that when we speak in a language given to us by the Holy Spirit, it may be a human language or one that angels speak, but whichever it is, it has meaning: in other words, it is a real language.

In her book, *The Helper*, Catherine Marshall tells a moving story of a shy pastor's wife in Indiana who felt compelled by the Spirit to pray aloud in tongues during a church service one summer's evening. The doors of Rosedale Church were open to keep the temperature down, so her words were heard by an elderly Greek miner who was passing by. The miner was sad and lonely, spending most of his time in the darkness and knowing no one outside his family who spoke Greek. So he was thrilled to hear someone speaking in his own native language. Not only that, but the stranger was telling him that God loved him and had a purpose for his life and wanted to bring joy and peace to him and to those he loved so dearly. He rushed into the church and began jabbering excitedly in Greek to the pastor's astonished wife. On learning the truth, he fell on his knees and gave his life to Christ. The following week his family joined him, and others came to believe in Christ too through what had happened.

What is the point of speaking in tongues?

When we speak in a language given by the Holy Spirit, it may be for one of several reasons.

(i) <u>We speak to God in private.</u>
Paul writes that the most common use of tongues is to address God directly in private prayer. (1 Corinthians 14:2,18,19)

This may be a prayer of worship, expressing our praise or thanks or love directly from our spirit to God. Worshipping in tongues enables us to express to him feelings and desires that we would find hard to put into our own words, and our spirit is strengthened as a result. (Acts 2:11; 1 Corinthians 14:4) Often, when I find it hard to pray, I begin by worshipping the Lord in tongues, and sometimes this turns into praise in tongues. After a short while I find I can pray more freely in my own language once more.

A second important use of tongues in private prayer is to intercede for people or situations when we don't know exactly how to pray for them. With tongues, we allow the Spirit to help us by giving us the words we need. Our own spirit supplies the faith and love and the desire for God to act; the Holy Spirit supplies the words. (Romans 8:26,27) Again, after interceding for a while in tongues, we may find that we then have a much clearer idea about how we should pray, so we can continue in our normal language.

(ii) <u>We bring a message from God to the church.</u>
This happens in the context of public worship. A message for the church in tongues needs someone to interpret it with the gift of interpretation so that everyone can understand it, unless of course it is addressed to someone present who speaks that language. (1 Corinthians 14:2-5,13) In general, it would be better to bring a

message from God in the language understood by the congregation, but to prophesy like this requires more faith than to speak in tongues. Nevertheless, having the courage to speak out in tongues can be a first step towards prophesying.

One potential value of speaking in a tongue in public is that it gives one or more other people an opportunity to exercise the gift of interpretation. It is always good when people can cooperate with each other in the Spirit.

More importantly, a message in tongues can set a service alight by encouraging other members of the congregation to speak out in the Spirit by sharing words of prophecy, visions, scriptures, exhortations or specific words of encouragement. It simply shakes things up!

Therefore, we should not hesitate in public worship to speak out in a tongue if we feel the Spirit is encouraging us to do so.

When you come together, each one has a hymn, a lesson, a revelation, a tongue, or an interpretation. Let all things be done for edification. If any speak in a tongue, let there be only two or at most three, and each in turn; and let one (or someone) interpret.   1 Corinthians 14:26,27

(iii) <u>We bring a message to a foreign language speaker in his own language.</u>

This could happen in church or in some other setting. When it does, it has a powerful effect on unbelievers, as it did on the Day of Pentecost and in the story of the Greek miner. It is what Paul was referring to in 1 Corinthians 14:21,22: '*In the law it is written, "By men of strange tongues and by the lips of foreigners I will speak to this people...." Thus, tongues are a sign not for believers but for unbelievers.*'

I once heard a Manchester pastor with no knowledge of French pray in that language in the power of the Holy Spirit. Knowing French, I could understand what he was saying, but we were in a worship service and there were no French people present, so apart from proving to me that tongues can be a genuine human language, this wasn't very helpful. However, I learned that he did this regularly, so perhaps the Spirit intended him to use this gift at some point for the benefit of genuine French speakers, and using it in church was merely practice. In that case, when I told him I understood what he was saying, my words would have been an encouragement to him.

Personally, I would love to bring a message from God supernaturally to a foreigner in his own tongue. I once tried to do this in a half-hearted way when I was staying in a youth hostel. I shared a dormitory with several East European men, so in the safety of the adjacent shower I sang in the Spirit, hoping they would hear me singing in their own language. Sadly, there was no response from them, not even a "Shutski upski!"

I suppose that if I really want to do this, I should be praying hard for an opportunity to do so. Paul tells us to desire earnestly the spiritual gifts and to pray for them. (1 Corinthians 14:1,13) A *genuine* desire for spiritual gifts is an important requirement for receiving them.

(iv) We pray for someone who is with us.

"My life would probably have taken a completely different turn without Ann's prayer for me in tongues all those years ago."

My wife's prayer in tongues for the lady who wrote those words helped to reunite the lady with God and bring her to life spiritually. If we are ministering to someone in person, and we don't know exactly how to pray or how to get started, then praying for them in tongues can open a channel for the Holy Spirit to work in a powerful way.

(v) We speak to demons.

This is probably a very rare use of tongues, but I did witness it once at a church meeting in west London. A woman was writhing about on the floor and hissing like a snake, clearly in the control of a demon. Two ministers tried unsuccessfully to cast it out, but it wouldn't leave until someone spoke to it fiercely in a tongue. At this the woman became still, then she stood up and spoke in her natural voice. The ministers were then able to counsel her and pray for her normally. Paul mentioned angelic languages, so perhaps the tongue was spoken in the demon's language, and that is why it then obeyed.

Can I be baptized in the Spirit and not speak in tongues?

I think you can be baptized in the Spirit without speaking in tongues, but what is the point? It would be rather like trying to use a paintbox without using the brush. That is possible, of course, but it is easier and better to use a brush, because that's the way a paintbox is meant to be used. Similarly, the Lord *expects* you to speak in tongues (Mark 16:17; 1 Corinthians 14:5); people who are baptized in the Holy Spirit *can* speak in tongues (Acts 2:4; 10:44-47; 19:6); and people who have been baptized in the Spirit nearly always *do* speak in tongues sooner or later. So why not you now?

The section headed 'Give the Holy Spirit control' in Chapter 4 explains why it is important to speak in tongues when you receive the Holy Spirit, and you have just been reading about the value of tongues, particularly in private prayer. If your human father wanted to give you a folding bicycle or a top-of-the-range smart phone or a fully automatic sewing machine, something very useful which you didn't have already, would you refuse it? So why refuse such a useful gift as tongues, when your heavenly Father longs to give it to you?

So why does St Paul forbid speaking in tongues?

He doesn't. He writes, '*Do not forbid speaking in tongues.*' (1 Corinthians 14:39) And he wrote, '*I thank God that I speak in tongues more than you all,*' so he could hardly have told the rest of us not to do it. (1 Corinthians 14:18)

Paul implied that he didn't speak in tongues himself during corporate worship, but he certainly didn't forbid it. He said that two or three people could bring a message in tongues, so long as someone was willing to interpret what they said for the benefit of everyone. (1 Corinthians 14:19,26,27)

This question is sometimes asked by people who have little understanding of Paul's teaching on spiritual gifts, or who have been incorrectly taught that the spiritual gifts ceased at the end of the apostolic age. So here is a quick summary of Paul's teaching on that whole subject in 1 Corinthians:

- In 12:7-10 he describes various *abilities* which the Holy Spirit gives to Christians to enable them to help others. These are clearly supernatural abilities which only the Holy Spirit gives, for the list includes 'gifts of healing', 'the working of miracles', and 'prophecy' for example. So 'various kinds of tongues' evidently means the supernatural ability to speak in different languages, not any naturally learned ability.
- In 12:28-30 he describes various *kinds of people* whom God provides to enable the church to do its job, and once again one of these is a person who speaks *'in various kinds of tongues* (languages)'.
- In chapter 13, he says that none of the gifts of the Spirit is exercised perfectly. All of them (e.g. prophecy, tongues and knowledge) will end 'when the perfect comes', for then they will no longer be needed. But for now, while we still need them, their use should be motivated by love for others and not for self-aggrandisement.
- In chapter 14:26-31, he describes various *ways* in which Christians can contribute to corporate worship. One way, he says, is by giving a message in a tongue, that is in words given by the Holy Spirit which the speaker himself does not understand. In this case, Paul says, someone should interpret it so that everyone may

Some questions about speaking in tongues 89

understand what has been said. The ability to interpret is another gift of the Holy Spirit.
- In 14:27-30,40 he says, '*If any speak in a tongue, let there be only two or at most three, and each in turn... Let two or three prophets speak, and let the others weigh what is said. If a revelation is made to another sitting by, let the first be silent... All things should be done decently and in order.*' In other words, whenever people are addressing the congregation there should not be too many of them, and they should speak one at a time.

We native Brits are so reserved! In Corinth, it seemed that everybody wanted to pitch in and have a say, whereas in a traditional British congregation, a preacher is lucky if he hears a muttered 'Amen' during his sermon. Next time you hear a preacher make a good point, try shouting out, "Preach it, bro'!" or "Preach it, sis!" I dare you!

Chapter 10: How can I continue to be filled with the Holy Spirit?

At times a Christian is more full of the Spirit than at other times. (Acts 4:8) We can be filled with the Spirit more than once. (Acts 4:31) Even in the life of Jesus, there were times when the power of the Spirit flowed through him more freely than at other times. (Luke 5:17) This is not to say that sometimes we have only a part of God's Spirit. *'It is not by measure that He gives the Spirit.'* (John 3:34) It's rather that at times the Spirit possesses more of us than he does at others.

God's Word tells us to continue to be filled with his Holy Spirit (Ephesians 5:18) This means repeatedly opening every part of our personality to the Spirit's direction and control. (Galatians 5:16,25) Being baptized in the Spirit is not a once and for all event, like being born again or ideally like getting married. Being filled with the Spirit, if I may say this without causing offence, is more like the act of married love. It needs to be renewed continually. Every Christian needs to receive the Holy Spirit, but it is even more important to be filled with the Spirit continually. I can think of ten ways to do this:

(i)   Praise God with all your heart in the company of other Christians. (Ephesians 5:18-20)
(ii) Worship God with spiritual gifts in the company of other Spirit-filled believers. (1 Corinthians 14:26-31)
(iii) Pray frequently for God to fill you with his Spirit and to give you power to do his will. (Acts 4:24-31)
(iv) Pray in tongues privately to build up your spiritual strength. (1 Corinthians 14:4)

(v) Read and meditate often on the words of God. (Luke 11:13; Acts 11:15; Galatians 3:2,5)

(vi) Don't grieve the Holy Spirit by resisting his leading, or by indulging in unholy thoughts, desires, words, or actions. Where necessary, seek reconciliation with your fellow believers. (Psalm 51:9-12; Ephesians 4:30-32)

(vii) Spend as much time as you can in intercession, praying for the salvation of the world, for fellow Christians, and especially for preachers of the gospel. (Luke 6:12,19; Ephesians 6:18-20)

(viii) Speak to people about Jesus Christ and his salvation. It is only as we need the Holy Spirit's power that we are given it. (Mark 13:10,11; Acts 4:8-12)

(ix) Seek by every spiritual means to overcome evil in whatever form you may find it. (Ephesians 6:12-18)

(x) Pray for gifts of the Spirit and look out for opportunities to use them in order to help other people in the love and power of God. (1 Corinthians 14: 1,3,13,16-19)

However, you cannot *keep* something until you *have* it. First you must receive God's promised gift of his Holy Spirit; then you can continue to be filled with the Spirit, as I've suggested above.

Practice makes perfect.

If you regularly pray in tongues in private, you may discover that God gives you different languages for different purposes – for praise, worship, intercession, binding and loosing, etc. As you grow in fluency, you will gain confidence for speaking or singing in tongues in corporate worship.

The same is true for prophecy. When you are alone in prayer, ask the Lord to speak to you in your own language, and then open your mouth and speak to yourself by faith in words the Spirit gives!

How can I continue to be filled with the Holy Spirit? 93

Years ago, when I knew the Lord had called me to serve him in Chile, I fasted for a day and then asked the Lord what he wanted me to do there. No voice or word of Scripture came into my head. So by faith, and trying not to think what I was saying, I spoke out what I trusted would be the Lord's answer to my question. What came out was a bit of a surprise. I was to be a key to unlock his resources in order to enable people to do things they would not otherwise have been able to do.

In Chile, God enabled me to bring people from different churches together in several evangelistic crusades, through which hundreds of people were saved and dozens were healed; and since then to found the charity Chile for Christ, which continues its work today.

Among many other achievements, Chile for Christ partially supported three pastors for many years and enabled their daughters to go to university; it helped to build eight proper houses in the foothills of the Andes for impoverished Pehuenche families, and it sent slightly used protective clothing and equipment worth around £90,000 new to two fire brigades whose volunteer crews would otherwise have had only what little they could afford to buy for themselves. The very first gift made was a bicycle for an aged pastor to enable him to visit his church members.

As with tongues, practising prophecy in private can be a first step towards prophesying in church or in conversation with unbelievers. Think about Jesus's conversation with the Samaritan women at the well of Sychar. (John 4:4-42) The Holy Spirit gave Jesus a prophetic word of revelation about the woman's life which broke through all her cultural barriers and convinced her that Jesus was God's promised Messiah. She excitedly introduced him to her village; he stayed with them for two days; *'and because of his words many more became believers.'* (John 4:41) All that through one prophetic sentence!

Like Jesus, we can receive revelation regarding people we talk to. God can give us a special word just for that person. By the power of the Holy

Spirit, we can speak words that can cause people to believe, just as Jesus himself did.

On the website truthortradition.com an article 'How to be a witness of Jesus, by Jesus' points out that Jesus's conversation with the Samaritan woman began when he was sitting down quietly to rest in a public place. It concludes with this advice:

> So set some time aside to go out and find a spot to relax. When you see someone coming your way, it could just be a person who needs to know Jesus. Don't rush into a dialogue on how to get saved. Instead, find out what they are interested in. Most importantly, follow Jesus' example and draw on the power available through the gift of Holy Spirit. Don't let cultural issues or prejudgements stop you from speaking what God would have you say.
>
> Our heavenly Father desires everyone to be saved and come to a knowledge of the truth (1 Timothy 2:4). Salvation comes through a knowledge of Jesus Christ. It's up to us to spread that knowledge, to be his witness. I think we can all continue to take his advice in John 4:35: "...open your eyes and look at the fields! They are ripe for the harvest."

Chapter 11: Ruled by the Spirit

In many churches, the Bible's teaching about these matters is not put into practice. In some churches it is actively rejected, in most others it is never even mentioned. There are many reasons for this: a desire by the leadership to maintain control over church services; a love of dead ritual; not taking the Bible seriously; not believing it; fear of the supernatural; fear of dividing the church; fear of deception; fear of being branded as crazy.

Some Christians are genuinely convinced that the supernatural work of the Holy Spirit ended with the death of the first apostles. In the 18th century Bishop Joseph Butler told John Wesley, *'The pretending to extraordinary revelations and gifts of the Holy Ghost is a horrid thing, a very horrid thing.'* Nevertheless, the belief that spiritual gifts ceased with the apostles is not based on the Bible. The Bible says they will cease only when 'the perfect comes', and both Christians and the world as a whole are still far from perfect. In his journal dated 15th August 1750, John Wesley wrote, *'The grand reason why the miraculous gifts were so soon withdrawn, was not only that faith and holiness were well-nigh lost; but that dry, formal, orthodox men began even then to ridicule whatever gifts they had not themselves, and to decry them all in others as either madness or imposture.'*

Jesus came to baptize us *all* in the Holy Spirit. (John 1:33) God declared through the prophet Joel that *all* his people would exercise supernatural gifts in these last days. (Joel 2:28,29) Jesus said that whoever who believed in him would do the things that he did, which included supernaturally healing the sick, discerning and casting out demons by the power of the Spirit, and prophesying. And he began that particular prophecy with the words, "Truly, truly." (John 14:12) We cannot say that the gifts of the Holy Spirit are not for us today if we take God's word seriously and if we want to remain in his will. So I'm going to finish this book by addressing why some churches and their leaders resist the Holy Spirit, to encourage you, if necessary, to think again. (Acts 7:51)

Fear

First, a word to individual Christians. In my teens I was taken to the top of a 40-foot-high parachute training tower. Fitting a harness on me, an instructor assured me that I could safely leap into space at a controlled speed. That was easier said than done! My instinct for self-preservation made it impossible for me to step off the tower until the instructor gave me a hard shove in the back. But once in the air I discovered I wasn't going to die after all: in fact, I felt great! I knew how birds must feel every day as they swoop and glide above us. I landed safely, as promised, and wanted to have another go!

Many people are afraid of flying in aeroplanes, but their fears usually wear off once they have summoned the courage to fly a few times. Others are afraid of public speaking. My knees were literally – yes literally – knocking together the first time I stood up to lead a church service, but my fear wore off with practice.

So it's not unusual to be afraid of launching out into a spiritual gift for the first time. To allow the Spirit to take control of what we are saying can seem frightening, and to speak out a word of prophecy in a church meeting or to lay hands on someone for healing can take courage. The same thing goes for sharing the Gospel with someone for the first time. Dare I open my mouth and start to speak about someone's eternal destiny? Will I simply embarrass both of us?

The only way to lose your fear of spiritual gifts is to put yourself into the hands of the Holy Spirit, launch out into space and fly! Everything gets easier with practice. Give it a go! You'll make mistakes, but that's better than never trying. Think how many mistakes little children make when they are learning to talk. But they would never learn to talk properly if they didn't keep trying. It's far better to try but fail, than to fail to try.

Disorder

People who feel that church services should be calm and dignified with only one person speaking at a time would feel anything from uncomfortable to horrified if they found themselves in a service where everyone was talking at once, or people were falling on the floor in trances, or others were speaking in languages that no one present could understand. Yet all these things took place in the life of the early church when it was growing rapidly. (Acts 4:24; Mark 9:25-27; Acts 19:6)

Similar things have happened during times of spiritual revival throughout the centuries. The American Presbyterian minister Charles Finney was credited with winning more than half a million souls to God during the nineteenth century. When he preached in one city, such fear gripped the congregation that one by one they fell to the ground. "If I had had a sword in each hand, I could not have cut them down as fast as they fell," he said. The meeting lasted all night long.

However, there is a time and place for everything that is of God. In normal times and in most cases, more ordered behaviour is appropriate. (Acts 22:1,2; 1 Corinthians 14:23-33) It is the responsibility of leaders to discern what is appropriate and what is not; what is of the Spirit of God and what is merely of men. We need leaders who can encourage the right use of spiritual gifts and discourage their misuse with gentleness, firmness and love.

Actually, God can order a meeting much better than we can if we will allow him to do so, provided that everyone in the congregation is sensitive to his Spirit and is eager to contribute to the meeting in order to help and encourage everyone else. The Holy Spirit can give to each person in turn some particular contribution to the worship, in a beautiful progression which man-made orders of service can rarely match. So don't reject the wonderful gifts of the Spirit merely because they have sometimes been misused. Pray for better leadership. As I wrote earlier, St Paul instructed his church members, *'My brethren, earnestly desire to prophesy, and do not forbid speaking in tongues; but all things should be done decently and in order.'* (1 Corinthians 14:39,40) Both parts of that sentence are important.

Division

Some church leaders avoid teaching about the baptism of the Spirit and encouraging the use of spiritual gifts for fear of bringing division in the church. But every time the Word of God is effectively proclaimed, it produces division. (John 7:43; 10:19; Hebrews 4:12) When the Word of God produces division among those who hear it, this is evidence that it is the Word of God. (Luke 12:49-53) The division between those who are truly seeking to know God and those who are not seeking him exists before the Word is preached; the preaching of the Word simply brings the division to light.

However, when God's Word is taught and practised within a church where everyone present loves God's truth and desires to do his will, this kind of division will not be produced. The only people who will reject it will be those who do not love the Lord enough to want to go along with his Word. (John 14:15) In time they will usually leave, so long as the leaders keep their hands on the tiller and resist changing course. (1 John 2:19)

Of course, there will be problems even in Spirit-filled churches. Wherever there is life, there are problems! A corpse doesn't have any problems, but who wants a corpse for a church? One reason leaders are needed is to deal with problems. Provided a church's leaders are united in their commitment to God's Word, especially as it relates to the ministry of the Holy Spirit, then the membership of the church will remain united too, and the church will grow!

Tradition

Much of what I have written in this book is contrary to the traditional teaching and practice of many churches. A church's traditions must always be judged by the Word of God, for the church exists to represent the Lord on earth, and it cannot do that if it is rebelling against him by contradicting his Word. Church leaders must continually check their teaching and behaviour against the Word of God, otherwise they will be like the scribes of Jesus's day, who *'made void the Word of God by the tradition of men.'* (Matthew 15:6; Mark 7:1-13)

Godly traditions are good, but human traditions can shackle us to the past and deafen us to what the Holy Spirit is saying in the present. When I was training for the ministry, a fellow student told us how as a local preacher he had gone to lead a service in a small rural chapel. Apart from him, there were only two people present: a lady representing the congregation, and the organist. When he announced the first hymn, he was astonished to see the congregational lady disappear behind the organ to pump it by hand, leaving him to sing alone!

Because I refused to practise infant baptism – a practice totally contrary to the purpose of baptism in the New Testament – I was told to leave the Methodist ministry after twelve years of relatively faithful service. I was going to be homeless and unemployed with a wife and four children to support. The Lord, however, wonderfully provided for our needs. Within a few months, and before my employment with the Methodist Church expired, I was appointed pastor of an evangelical free church, with a house built especially for a family of six like ours. Our God is wonderfully faithful: he never lets us down! So it was a good outcome for me, but I am immensely sad that a denomination which had 487,972 members in the UK shortly before I left it in 1981 now in 2021 has less than 170,000 members, a loss of two-thirds in a single generation.

The apostles said, *"We must obey God rather than men."* (Acts 5:29) Every detail in which a denomination's traditional practices and teaching are not in accordance with the will of God as expressed in his written Word should be changed until they are.

Formality

The original *Book of Common Prayer* for the Church of England was published in 1549 in the reign of King Edward VI. Its authors had the magnificent vision of uniting the whole of England in common prayer and the reading of God's Word, so that every Sunday everyone in the land would listen to the same Bible passages for that week and would approach God with the same prayers of confession and penitence, and with the same petitions and supplications both for their own good and the good of the nation as a whole.

Evidently, my description of biblical worship in Chapter 6 is in almost total contrast to worship as envisaged by Edward VI and Archbishop Thomas Cranmer. Equally, it has almost nothing in common with a sung Eucharist led by a cathedral choir, or the service of nine lessons and carols sung each Christmas in the chapel of King's College, Cambridge, accompanied by a full pipe organ with four keyboards and some fifty stops!

So is the corporate worship described in the New Testament the only way God wants us to worship him, or is it just one of various ways to worship him, from which we are free to choose according to our personal preference?

St Paul described corporate worship in the early days of the church. *'When you come together, each one has a hymn, a lesson, a revelation, a tongue, or an interpretation.'* (1 Corinthians 14:26) Compared with more formal kinds of church service, this is the difference between attending an orchestral concert and playing in the orchestra; or between watching a football match and playing in it. It is true that football supporters who attend a match do get involved in it to some extent. They applaud good play and shout encouragement (or abuse). They may even sing together when things are going well. But it's not the same as playing in the team itself and contributing actively to its victory.

So are the more formal ways of worship wrong? No, of course not. There is value in just attending a football match or a concert, and there is value in attending any kind of church service that does not by its nature contradict the truth of God's Word. But I would liken the worship in most traditional churches, at least in the West, to worship under the Old Covenant. Under the Old Covenant worshippers brought their offerings to the priests, but it was the priests who offered them to God and conducted the associated rituals and prayers, while the worshippers remained as onlookers. In the New Covenant we are all called to be priests. (1 Peter 2:9)

Actually, the services of Morning Prayer and Evening Prayer in the Anglican prayer book are a kind of half-way house, in that worshippers do at least say together various prayers of confession, thanksgiving, petition and praise, and even the Apostles' Creed. So it's sad that the use of such prayers has been completely dropped in many Anglican churches in Britain. Nevertheless, even these traditional services fall short of worship in which everyone can contribute something which the Spirit gives them for the common good.

I confess that I disliked playing football at school. (I am talking about soccer, not American football, in which the players seem to use their hands more than their feet.) In those days the positions on a football field included left back and right back. My own preferred team position was left out! When I did play, my efforts to keep away from the ball in case I did something stupid with it usually hindered rather than helped. Accordingly, in a church which does allow everyone to contribute, everyone should come prepared to participate actively and enthusiastically rather than stand on the sidelines. Come to a service prepared to be a blessing, and not merely to be blessed!

Yesterday, as I write this section, I told the Lord I was willing to contribute something to the morning's worship if he would give me something to say. Arriving at the church car park, I prayed again. Some words of the prophet Malachi came to mind: *"Put me to the test, says the Lord."* When the service leader invited people to contribute something they believed God had given them, I brought this word to the church. I said I thought it meant that there was someone who believed God wanted him to do something or possibly to say something to someone, but was afraid that God might not enable him to do it. I said I believed God was saying, "Put me to the test. Do what I've told you to do, and you'll find that I won't fail you." The service leader himself immediately said, "That was a word from God for me."

If we want to enjoy God's very best, then being led and empowered by the Holy Spirit is how we should live every part of our life, including our worship of him.

Epilogue

The Lord doesn't want us to live in the past. He wants us to live in the present, preparing ourselves and the world for the cataclysmic events to come in the near future. Soon Jesus will return, as a bridegroom comes for his chosen bride. When he comes, he longs to find his church perfect, *'without spot or blemish or any such thing'*, living in every way just as he has desired. The Lord Jesus is pleading with his people, saying again and again to you and me, *"Hear what the Spirit is saying to the churches."* (Ephesians 5:25; Revelation 2:7,11,17,29; 3:6,13,22)

Let's embrace everything the Holy Spirit has revealed to us, and receive eagerly all that he wants to give us. His gifts are to make us strong in faith and hope and love; his presence in us is to make us holy. We need his help! It is the Holy Spirit who glorifies Jesus and draws people to him. It is the Holy Spirit who convinces the world of sin and righteousness and judgement. It is the Holy Spirit who gives us the power we need to be effective witnesses to the resurrection and to the eternal life which is promised to all who put their trust in Jesus. Spiritual revival, which our nation so desperately needs, can begin only with a revival of the Spirit.

Jesus longs to be united with a holy, Spirit-filled bride. *'Christ loved the church and gave himself up for her, that he might sanctify her, having cleansed her by the washing of water with the word, that he might present the church to himself in splendour, without spot or wrinkle or any such thing, that she might be holy and without blemish.'* (Ephesians 5:25-27) He will be fully satisfied only when the bride for whom he died is living in every respect as he desires.

❧   ❧   ❧   ❧   ❧   ❧   ❧   ❧

A prayer to be born again

Dear Lord Jesus,
I believe you are the Son of God. You know who I am. I realize that because of my sin, I am under a death sentence. I am truly sorry for all the wrong things I have done and said and thought. (If there's anything in particular on your conscience, mention it now.) Please forgive me. With your help, I now want to live the way you want me to and to fulfil the purpose you made me for.
Lord Jesus,
I thank you very, very much that you died on the cross, so that I can be forgiven and set free from sin to live forever in your kingdom. I now give my life back to you. Please be my Saviour and Lord, and help me to live for you from this moment onwards.
Thank you, Lord Jesus.

The prayer above is not a prayer to be filled with the Holy Spirit. I think it is better to ask your church leaders or trusted Christian friends to pray with you rather than pray on your own for the Holy Spirit, and then only if you have publicly demonstrated your repentance from sin and faith in Christ through baptism by immersion, in accordance with Biblical practice. Nevertheless, God has sometimes answered a private prayer with a mighty infilling of his Spirit, so if he has given you the faith to ask him right now, go ahead: I won't try to stop you!

※ ※ ※ ※ ※ ※ ※ ※

If you found this book helpful, please recommend it to your friends. Also, please, *please* write some comments about it on its page at Amazon or another online bookseller, or on a book review website. Most people will buy a book online from an unfamiliar author only if it has lots of positive feedback from other readers.

Epilogue

Folk hesitate to buy a book that no one else has read,
But if it has some good reviews, then they might go ahead!

I have written this book to encourage and motivate the church to recover the fullness of life in the Spirit, for the sake of those who are not yet saved. So I want as many people as possible to read it! Please do whatever you can to help.

To see other books I've written, visit www.booksforlife.today.

God bless you!

Other books by Arnold V Page

God, Science and the Bible
URLink Print & Media, LLC, 2020.
ISBN 978-1-64753-2993299-4
Also available in Spanish.
Books for Life Today, 2021.
ISBN 978-1-91612-138-6
Which is right: science or the Bible? With fact-based science and original and convincing logic, *God, Science and the Bible* presents in a straightforward way the truth about: the big bang theory – the theory of evolution – the age of the universe – Noah's flood – the fossil record – and the age of ancient trees. It answers the questions: does God exist? - is the Bible true? - did Jesus really live, die and return to life? - can we live for ever, and if so, how?

"This is a brilliant book and definitely one I will recommend to friends. 'God, Science and the Bible' asks and answers the questions we have all wondered about but maybe never found the answer to. This book was fascinating. I couldn't put it down." Helen Lawrence, Amazon Reviewer

Z: The Final Generation
Westbow Press
ISBN 978-1-9736-3021-0
What does the future hold for Generation Z, the current crop of children and young people? Nothing less than the most exciting event in history! In this controversial and powerfully argued book, researcher and Bible teacher Arnold V Page contends that Z, the final letter of the alphabet, will also be the final generation that grows to adulthood before

Jesus Christ returns to establish justice, peace and righteousness throughout the earth.

"*A well-researched and brilliantly articulated work.*"
Ruffina Oserio, ReadersFavorite.com

"*It's a gift of faith, one that should be read and passed on.*"
Romuald Dzemo, ReadersFavorite.com

Z: Answers for the Final Generation

Westbow Press, 2018.

ISBN 978-1-9736-3023-4

How can the Bible be correct when it tells us that the world is only 6,000 years old? Does the fossil record really support the theory of evolution? Was Jesus mistaken when he said that he would return within the lifetime of his hearers? Will believers in Jesus finally live in heaven or on earth? In this sequel to his controversial and challenging book, *Z: The Final Generation*, research scientist and theologian Arnold V Page answers these and other questions with original and convincing logic.

"*A fascinating and challenging book for anyone interested in end time events.*"
Darin Godby, ReadersFavorite.com

The Destiny of the Damned

The Open Bible Trust, 2018.

ISBN 978-1-78364-447-6

"How can a God of love deliberately torment unbelievers forever in hell, especially if they have never heard of Jesus?" That is a question many Christian writers fail to address. However, in this book Arnold V Page faces it head on by showing, from the pages of Scripture, that God does not do such a thing, and that everlasting torment is not the fate of unbelievers. Indeed, some of them will have their names written in the Book of Life.

Other books by Arnold V Page

Twenty-First Century Nutrition and Family Health
New Generation Publishing, January 2015.
ISBN 978-1-78507-177-5
Obtainable post free in the UK from booksforlife.today.
Eighty years ago, the rampant epidemics of obesity, coronary heart disease and Type 2 diabetes hardly existed. So why did they start? And why does no one seem able to bring them to an end? *Twenty-First Century Nutrition and Family Health* finally provides the answers.

"My wife and I have put a lot of this book's food advice into practice, and I've also taken the advice about exercise. I've got my weight down to the middle of my BMI range, stopped taking two different medicines (with my GP's approval, of course), one for cramps and one for stomach aches, and am feeling much, much better for it. Every family should have a copy. I bought copies for my children."
                                                                 Rev. Gregory Hargrove, JP
"I'm very impressed. Brilliant!"   Dr David Walton MBBS

Unearthly Passion – a novel for New Adults
Vincy Page (pen name). Books for Life Today, October 2020.
ISBN 978-1-91612-130-0 (paperback)
ISBN 978-1-91612-131-7 (Epub)
ASIN B08BW872H7 (Mobi)
ASIN B08DYGN7RX (Spoken Realms audiobook)
Unwanted and unloved as a child, Natalie Parsons longs to escape from the moral restraints of her foster family and embark on a life of boozing and floozing at Edinburgh University. Her first-year geophysics course finds her rebelling against the idea that the universe created itself. Longing for love and a sense of identity, she drifts ever deeper into drink, debt and depravity until she hits a rock that sinks her in a life-threatening depression. Rescue comes through a friend who claims to know God, producing a dilemma that only a miracle can solve.

"This is a great book for those getting ready to leave home and head for university. It makes you think about what really matters when pressures come from every angle."

Will Samson, Amazon reviewer

"I only wish that every pastor, parent, teacher, social worker and indeed anyone interested in truth and morality, as I am, would read this excellent book."

Rev. Gregory Hargrove, JP

About the author

Arnold V Page, BSc(Eng), BD, MIWSc, AIMMM, has been a Methodist minister in the UK and Chile, the pastor of an evangelical church in Buckinghamshire, and the senior engineer in a company specializing in research and design related to timber building structures. At the age of 70 he climbed all sixteen 3000-ft peaks in Snowdonia in 24 hours, having previously completed the Three Peaks Challenge, also within 24 hours. Now nearly 80 years old, he continues to keep fit, using the principles and methods described in his book, *Twenty-First Century Nutrition and Family Health.*

Arnold's wife and best friend Ann died in 2019, and he now spends most of his time writing Christian books. He is a member of Elim Hope Church in the Buckinghamshire village of Lane End, and he has four children and three grandsons.

Tell me about the Holy Spirit

www.ingramcontent.com/pod-product-compliance
Lightning Source LLC
Chambersburg PA
CBHW071523080526
44588CB00011B/1539